I0421318

Faith, SUPERNATURAL BELIEFS, AND OUR SYMBOLIC BRAIN

HERMAN KAGAN, PH.D.

Copyright © 2013 Herman Kagan
All rights reserved.
ISBN-10: 1482028050
ISBN-13: 9781482028058
Library of Congress Control Number: 2013901198
CreateSpace Independent Publishing Platform
North Charleston, SC

PREFACE

At a teacher's conference for Emily, who is in kindergarten, Ms. Jorden says to Emily's mother, "I think it's time you let Emily know that the Tooth Fairy and Cinderella do not really exist, because she keeps talking about them as if they were real people. I believe it's important for children to know the difference between fantasy and reality." Emily's mother, Mrs. Grey, tells Ms. Jorden that there is time enough to puncture Emily's fantasy world and that she'll do this when she thinks Emily is ready. "I think she's old enough now," voices Ms. Jorden. Mrs. Grey replies, "There are adults who still believe that angels exist and it hasn't done them any harm." Ms. Jorden now realizes that she is in for a debate and makes the first strike by telling Emily's mother that the Bible proclaims that angels do exist but says nothing about the Tooth Fairy or Cinderella. Mrs.Grey counters by remarking that not everything in the Bible can be taken literally and some of the stories and actions of the biblical characters are meant to be metaphors. After this exchange they both begin to realize that neither one is going to come out ahead and they depart with a friendly "thank you" and "goodbye."

As a psychologist I realize that our brain can hold on to both fantasy and reality at the same time and that sometimes it's hard to know which is which. Belief in reincarnation, an afterlife, and astrology are prime examples. This dilemma intrigued me and made me wonder why people hold on to supernatural beliefs or seek supernatural paths. From a historical perspective, supernatural beliefs have been with us since recorded history and even before. From an evolutionary perspective, it appears that supernatural beliefs may have been a way to deal with anxiety, fear, and stress and thus favored by natural selection. My book, in fact, looks at the supernatural from both a historical and an evolutionary perspective and answers the question of why supernatural beliefs continue to exist in the twenty-first century.

This required research into the accepted beliefs of ancient Egypt, Greece, China, and India and whether any of these beliefs are still accepted. I tried to tackle the project by imagining how people handled physical illnesses and what cures were offered, and whether their trust and faith in their healers played a part in their recovery and survival. People did survive long before medical science made its appearance, so it was and still is important to know what affected their recovery and survival. How well I imagined the people in the ancient world rests with the readers of the book, but I believe I did a pretty good job. I am sure that people who are interested in speculating why supernatural beliefs continue in this century would learn much from reading this book. Its novel approach and conclusions would befit the intellectual pursuits of readers who want to take on the challenge of understanding how our brain determines what is fiction and what is nonfiction. Sometimes this is not an easy task, but it is worthwhile.

ACKNOWLEDGMENTS

I would like to thank the many people who were willing to read and give me feedback about the rough drafts of the book by writing down their evaluations, correcting mistakes, and making encouraging remarks that helped me keep going. Some, like me, plodded through, chapter by chapter, and some gave me specific information about questions that came up. Others just offered an opinion about the book's content.

Family members, colleagues, and friends all pitched in to help. My wife, Verna, a busy attorney managing the pro bono program for the county bar association, was the first one, who was always willing and ready to read the first draft of every chapter and to give her opinion about its strengths and weaknesses. Then came Louise Ross, my cousin, who is the Publication Coordinator for the Joslyn Center, who corrected spelling mistakes and sentence structure and told me whether or not the content held her interest. My son Ken, who is a CPA and owns his own business—along with his partner Ed Costello—helped me out with a percentage question that was relevant to the premise of the book, and my daughter added her opinion about the book's content when I first began writing. Two of my psychological colleagues, Gil McFarlane, who is a Senior Psychologist at Ventura County Behavioral Health, and Richard Reinhart, formerly Chief Psychologist at Ventura County Behavioral Health and now in private practice, were very helpful in their critiques of the psychological premises and conclusions throughout the book and spent many hours going over all eight chapters. I certainly appreciated their input. And one of my childhood friends, Ronald Massarik, who practiced internal medicine and is now a retired physician, willingly read several chapters and provided feedback about the medical aspects of the book's contents. In addition, a neighbor, Brad Guzikowski, who was enrolled in a psychology course at the local junior college, provided a student's viewpoint of the first two chapters.

Finally, the students in the Secular Student Alliance group at Northern Arizona University, under the leadership of Miles Schneiderman, provided feedback on how well the contents fit the premises involved, whether their belief in atheism could be reconciled with the book's conclusions, and how interesting they found the book.

The various perspectives from all the people involved in looking over the book's premises and content kept me on the right path and allowed Eric Larson, who has a business in Santa Barbara called Studio e Books, to edit *Faith, Supernatural Beliefs and Our Symbolic Brain* before sending it to be published. Much appreciation goes to him for the professional job that he did.

TABLE OF CONTENTS

INTRODUCTION

The world as we know it is not a symbolic one. When a tornado is headed toward a city, weather forecasters don't say, "based on the tornado's actions it looks to be only making a symbolic gesture and should do no actual damage," or when a bear is headed toward your table, which is loaded with food, a ranger nearby is not apt to say "don't panic, the bear looks like he's only making a symbolic gesture." The world we are exposed to has stars, oceans, rivers, volcanoes, trees, and hurricanes. It is also full of life, with different species interacting with each other. Some are predators, like hawks, eagles, and wolves, and others are non-predators that attack only nuts and berries. We are part of this world and are conscious of how vast and complicated it is. However, it is a world full of actual items, not symbolic ones, and astronomers have yet to describe the "big bang" as a symbolic event as opposed to a real one.

While it took evolution billions of years to accomplish, we have been endowed with a brain that understands, creates, and communicates in symbolic terms. This has led to children picking up and speaking one or more languages at an early age and learning to read, do math, and create artwork in grade school. So we are put in a non-symbolic world and yet we have to understand and explain it with symbolic models and formulas that can be passed down to our children. This is unique to human beings. Indeed, we think, create, and communicate symbolically. Our brain is programmed this way. It has allowed us to create symbolic systems like language, mathematics, musical notation, and other artistic creations. There seems to be no end to what we can imagine and create.

Natural selection has seen fit to view our symbolic brain in a favorable light. It has allowed us to produce and distribute food, kill with weapons of our creation, build shelters, travel anywhere in the world, develop medical systems that take care of pregnant women and newborn babies, and create societies that sustain our lives and property. This bodes well for our reproductive sustainability and our continued survival.

However, there is another side to this positive story about our symbolic brain. It is open to reality and nonfiction as well as to fantasy and fiction. Our imagination can solve problems or take us on a wild ride to Neverland. It is boundless in its creativity and takes in both our real and dream worlds. It can go astray and produce illusions, delusions, and hallucinations. Our not-too-distant past is full of myths, legends, magical beliefs, false models, and racist stereotypes. And what we believe has profound effects on our health, well-being, and future. So, the picture of our symbolic brain seems to be both positive and negative.

As one can see, it is not always easy to distinguish between the real and the fanciful ideas and models that our symbolic brain creates, because what we believed three thousand or even three hundred years ago has radically changed. We no longer believe the earth is flat, that we are the center of the universe, or that illness is caused by demons who enter our bodies or by an angry god.

Yet the same questions that confronted us before about what is real and not real keep popping up. Do ghosts really exist; is there an afterlife; can prayer cure disease; can we communicate with the dead; will we reunite with dead family members after we die; is there a God who knows we are here and cares about us; and are there other, similarly intelligent creatures in the universe?

From an evolutionary standpoint, we could ask, if animals couldn't distinguish between reality and fantasy, how long would they last? Probably not very long, unless the fantasies had some survival value. This to my mind is a major question. Does our belief in the supernatural have any survival value? Does it help us in any way and if it does, in what way? My book attempts to answer these questions by looking at our innate nature, our past beliefs, our myths, and how our symbolic brain functions. And it reaches a conclusion. My hope is that you'll reach the same one.

CHAPTER I

Signs, Signals, and Symptoms in Animals and Man

Becoming Alert

On July 29, 2008, I was in the kitchen of my home making some toast for my breakfast. Standing next to the counter on which the toaster rested, I suddenly felt as if I were standing on an unstable, shifting floor. Or was the floor stable and I shifting? I wasn't sure which one it was. I began to wonder if I was having a dizzy spell or another episode of vertigo like the one I had had some time ago. And then I noticed that the curtains on the sides of the kitchen window were swaying back and forth. This made me realize that it was the ground that was shifting and not I, and that an earthquake was taking place. The shifting floor and swaying curtains, taken together, were the signs my mind needed to be convinced that an earthquake was underway. My conviction was confirmed when I turned on the radio and heard that an earthquake had just hit in the greater Los Angeles area near the city of Chino Hills in San Bernardino County.

Sometimes survival depends upon knowing what signs and signals to look for when disaster strikes. The Moken people of Thailand—known as the Sea Gypsies—were virtually unknown to the outside world until the 2004 tsunami hit Southeast Asia. While they have no written language and no recorded history, their grandparents and parents had passed down an important message based on past experience with the sea. They knew a receding sea was a sign or signal that a tsunami was on its way. They all took refuge in the mountains, and they all survived—unlike the thousands of people along the coast who perished, not knowing that a receding sea was a sign of a coming tsunami.[1]

Unlike traditional peoples with their natural signs and signals, city-dwellers are beset by beeping horns, howling sirens, flashing lights, traffic signals, turn signals, car alarms, smoke alarms, alarm clocks, cell phone tunes, whistling tea kettles, gas smells, and barking dogs. There are also signals and symptoms from our bodies that protrude into our consciousness. Feeling energetic, feeling tired, getting hunger pangs, becoming thirsty, becoming nauseous, needing to go to the bathroom, feeling pain, experiencing anxiety, and feeling ill are among the many signs and symptoms with which we become familiar as we mature. We then have the task of making our children more and more aware of the same urban and bodily signs, signals, and symptoms.

Built-In Programs

If you own a pet, you become aware of all the places it wants to sniff and explore. With acute senses of smell and hearing, animals are programmed to pay attention to signs and signals that pertain to their survival, physical well-being, and freedom of movement. Bring out a leash, and your dog knows this is a sign or signal that it's time to go for a walk. If there's a tree around, or the scent of another animal, the dog will stop, sniff, and leave its own deposit to mark its territory. Sometimes a dog will find a scent and follow it in tracking behavior. With their keen sensitivity to signals, dogs can be trained to guide blind people across busy streets, detect illegal drugs, find buried bodies, and sense when a person is about to have an epileptic seizure. Their keen senses can also be a detriment in our noise-filled society. I once owned a German shepherd who would run and hide whenever he heard a loud, sharp noise like a car backfiring, a cap pistol going off, or exploding fireworks. If this dog was ever in a forest and a gunshot went off, he would find a hiding place where nobody would easily find him. This might serve as a survival strategy for a wild dog, but it wasn't very good in a city full of booms, bangs, and backfiring cars. Throughout the three and a half billion years that life has been on earth, organisms have evolved the ability to sense and respond to signs and signals from the external environment and from their own bodies, which increases their chances of survival. This is true for both one-celled organisms and for humans. For example, a report from the Science Library at the University of Albany on how bacteria use signals states:[2]

> Instead of language, bacteria use signalling molecules which are released into the environment. As well as releasing the signaling molecules, bacteria are able to measure the number (concentration) of the molecules within a population. Nowadays we use the term "Quorum Sensing" (QS) to describe the phenomenon

whereby the accumulation of signalling molecules enables a single cell to sense the number of bacteria (cell density).

QS enables bacteria to co-ordinate their behavior. As environmental conditions often change rapidly, bacteria need to respond quickly in order to survive. It is very important for pathogenic bacteria during infection of a host (e.g., humans, other animals, or plants) to coordinate their virulence in order to escape the immune response of the host in order to be able to establish a successful infection.

Recognition of Self and Non-Self

Detecting and sending signals are two fundamental activities of all life. One of the basic signals or signs that living organisms search for is whether another organism is the same as or different from itself. This hunt for sameness was recently discussed in the journal *Science* with regard to bacteria living in colonies: they formed boundaries between colonies of different strains but merged with other colonies of the same strain. The authors state that in order to form these boundaries, bacteria must be able to discriminate between self and non-self groups, and that certain genes provide them with the means of decoding chemical signals that allow them to make this distinction.[3]

Discrimination between self and non-self is also performed by the guardians of ant colonies. Like the bacteria, the guards depend on reading chemical signals that other ants exude. One study suggests that ants rub their antennae over each other to determine whether they are self or non-self members.[4] James F. Lynch, a zoologist at the Chesapeake Bay

Center for Environmental Studies, names two other ways that ants stop non-self members from entering their homes. One species of carpenter ant makes its nest in hollow plant stalks or tree limbs, in which small entry holes have been made. The colony raises guard ants whose heads, "shaped like bottle corks," exactly fit the holes. The guards plug the entrances with their heads and will not withdraw until a returning colony member gives a tactile signal to identify itself. A second method of keeping out intruders depends on recognizing the odor of the ant colony in which an individual resides, since colonies have distinct identifying odors.[5] Without the ability to detect and transmit signals, the colony's survival would be short-lived.

Since we humans live in a world teeming with microorganisms, we have been provided with a biological immune system—thanks to evolution and natural selection—that also depends on the process of discriminating between self and non-self entities in order to protect our body from invading pathogens. This ability is basic to our survival, and has been basic to the survival of all forms of life. The medical profession has to take this survival mechanism into account when it attempts to transplant organs from one individual into another, since the immune system attempts to destroy non-self material. The similarity between the way we protect our bodies from intruders and the way bacteria and ants protect their colonies is a sobering thought when contemplating our supposed uniqueness. We all face similar challenges and nature has provided similar responses to help us survive.

The Process of Association

The ability to detect and respond to the signs, signals, and symptoms that alert us to danger underlies our power to protect, preserve, and enhance our life and physical well-being, as well as our property and possessions. And we comprehend the danger by its emotional impact on us.[6] Take the process of conditioning that the Russian physiologist Ivan Pavlov discovered with dogs. They first salivated when powder was put into their mouths, then they started salivating at the mere sight of the food and, later, at the sight of the assistant who brought the food, and then at the sound of the assistant's footsteps.[7] The ability to associate a given sign or signal with a particular outcome is one that children develop early on and it persists throughout life. A child associates a white dog with a loud startling noise several times, and soon the white dog becomes a frightening animal. This can even spread to other white animals or other white objects. It can even develop into a phobia.[8]

In fact, this process of association is at the heart of science, which investigates cause and effect. The sun sets and the sky gets dark; we see smoke and then we see fire; we put pure sodium in water and an explosive reaction takes place; astronomers look at the stars and galaxies and notice they are retreating every day and every year that they are observed. Medicine and psychology also use the process of association to attribute certain symptoms with certain diseases. Diagnoses stem from such associations. For example, severe abdominal pain initiates a search for a diagnosis that includes an analysis of temperature, blood pressure, pulse rate, and urine composition, followed by X-rays. If nothing specific can be diagnosed, physicians start thinking about psychological causes.

This is in fact what transpired when I took my wife to the emergency room of a local hospital. An on-call physician, after performing an examination and finding no physical cause, prescribed a tranquilizer to help her with the psychological stress that he assumed was causing the pain. I knew how my wife responded to stress, and this was not one of the ways, as far as I was concerned. I kept calling—it was after hours—and I finally got hold of one of the partners of my wife's primary physician. He met us in the emergency room and ordered an abdominal X-ray and a blood test. After looking at the results, he concluded that she had an intestinal obstruction. A surgeon who specialized in abdominal surgery was located, and she was operated on at two a.m. in a life-saving procedure. Once again, knowing what signs, signals, and symptoms to look for can mean the difference between surviving and not surviving.

Diagnosing psychological disorders also depends on recognizing symptoms and determining if they fall into normal or abnormal behavior patterns. Take the diagnosis of a compulsive disorder for individuals who overdo shopping or gambling. The clinician has to decide if: (1) the person feels driven to perform the activity; (2) the behavior is aimed at reducing distress or preventing some dreaded event or situation; (3) the person recognizes that his behavior is excessive or unreasonable; (4) the behavior significantly interferes with the individual's normal routine, occupational functioning, or social relationships; and (5) the disturbance is not due to drugs or a medical condition.[9] Unlike the medical tests that pinpoint abnormalities in blood cells or intestinal function, the diagnosis of psychological disorders depends on looking at behavior and judging when it has become excessive, interferes with so-called normal functioning, or produces distress. So, when a given behavior is defined as a clinical symptom depends to a great extent on whether the behavior is considered distressful or disturbing.

Making Models and Using Signals

The principle of cause-and-effect is the conceptual foundation of science and its various branches including astronomy, chemistry, biology, medicine, and psychology. After observing certain sequences of events over and over again, experiments are performed that break the events into smaller pieces. This helps to understand the sequences in more detail. The goal is to come up with a conceptual model that explains observations, has predictive power, and can help with human endeavors. Some of the most famous conceptual models are Einstein's equation $E=mc^2$, Watson and Crick's double-helix model of DNA, and Darwin's theory of evolution. Humans seem to be driven by a never-ending quest to make new discoveries and find out how things work.

I believe the motivation for this comes from our built-in need to protect, preserve, and enhance the lives, possessions, and identity of ourselves and those individuals and groups we love or are bonded with. We also want to know if life exists elsewhere in the universe, so astronomers send signals out into space in hopes of reaching other life forms, who will detect the signals and send back their own replies. Just as bacteria use signal-detection and communication to find out whether any comrades are around in their host, our most educated astronomers use signal-detection and communication to find out whether any comrades are around in the universe—which can be considered our host.

Built-in and Learned Sensing and Responding

Throughout the plant and animal kingdoms, responses to certain signals seem to be built in. When a fly gets caught in a spider web and struggles to escape, the vibrations produce an immediate and orchestrated response from the spider. The Venus Flytrap responds to insects landing on its leaves and stimulating its sensitive hairs by folding its leaves and trapping them.

A recent report in *Science* informs us that in threatening situations the secretion of alarm pheromones is widely used throughout both the plant and animal kingdoms. The most recently discovered location for pheromone secretion in mice is at the tip of the nose. The authors state that "pheromonal communication plays an important role in social interactions among individuals of the same species, affecting in particular sexual, territorial, and maternal behaviors." They conclude that sensitivity to alarm pheromones is present both in primitive organisms such as worms and in humans as well.[10]

Smell is crucial to the survival of many animals, especially those in frigid territories. Reindeer, for example, have such a keen sense of smell that they can detect plants that are buried under the snow and can pinpoint the location of a mushroom one hundred yards away.[11]

Even at home we can see that signs and signals are widely used. For example, a variety of wild birds come into my backyard to use the feeder, and something heard or seen sends them off all at once in a mass movement, as if they were tethered together. The postman comes to deliver the mail, and all my dogs are at the front door barking their heads off as if he were a threat.

Of course, many signals are learned through the process of association, as when dogs learn that taking out a leash is a signal that they are about to be taken for a walk, and when children learn that a certain tune coming from the street is a signal for the approach of the ice-cream man. Adults have learned to be aware of the smell of gas leaking from their stoves and that a continuous beep, beep, beep late at night is connected to an annoying car alarm going off somewhere nearby.

Missing an Important Signal

I remember an experience my wife and I had when we were living in a rented house while I was going to graduate school at the University of Arizona in Tucson. We owned a dog named Buddy, who was friendly with a dog down the street called Sally. Sally's owner would allow her to visit us on her own and she and Buddy would play together until supper time; then we would send Sally home by pointing her in the right direction and saying quite loudly, "Go!" This was enough to send her back. Well, one evening, long after supper, we heard barking outside our house, and lo and behold there was Sally. We yelled at her to go back home, but she didn't respond and kept barking. We kept yelling and she kept barking, so we went out and pushed her in the direction of her home and encouraged her to return home in no uncertain terms. She reluctantly started back home, then turned around as if to come back, but we kept insisting she go back home. We finally succeeded in sending her home, but we wondered why she had been so persistent in getting our attention at such a late hour. Our wondering was answered the next day, when we found out that the woman who owned Sally had been held at knife-point by an intruder who tied her up and robbed her house. Apparently Sally had been sending us a signal that something was wrong—a signal that we ignored. To this day, I regret not paying more attention to Sally's persistent barking. I responded to it as something annoying rather than as an alerting message.

Sexual Readiness Signals

In retrospect, signals have been used by living organisms for their survival since the beginning of life, which goes back some three and a half billion years—a billion years after the earth was formed. Protection, preservation, and enhancement of life and physical well-being have been served well by the use of signals, signs, and symptoms. While protection of the body is an evolutionary imperative, life couldn't continue without reproduction. Sexual signaling has therefore become an important part of mating and reproduction.

A report given by veterinarian Karen Overall at the Atlantic Coast Veterinary Conference held in Atlantic City, New Jersey, highlighted the extent to which non-verbal signaling is used by all social vertebrates to indicate sexual desire and readiness as well as to negotiate other social interactions.

Visual, tactile, vocal, olfactory, and pheromonal signals are all used. Dr. Overall stressed the importance of realizing that signaling involves a set of rules that will be shaped by the evolutionary history of the species.[12]

The courtship and mating rituals of birds are great examples of the variety, timing, duration, and holding power of signals. Singing, color displays, aerial acrobatics, rhythmic drumming, aggressive actions, and courtship feeding are just a few of the ways male birds try to attract mates.

Once a male produces his arsenal of pay-attention-to-me signals, it is up to the female to accept or reject the suitor in question. Tanagers and orioles are noted for their brilliant color displays; mockingbirds can keep up their lyrical songfest all night long; woodpeckers drum with their bills on dead limbs; nighthawks dive down toward their prospective mates, producing a booming sound; and the marsh hawk's aerial dips and somersaults are well known by bird watchers. The courtship dance of the whooping crane is performed by both males and females, each bowing to its mate, leaping high in the air with its wings flapping, and then bounding up and down. In courtship feeding the male places the food he has collected—insects, berries, fishes, nuts, seed, or whatever—directly into the open mouth of the female, and this apparently acts as a kind of sexual stimulant; males of the yellow-billed cuckoo, for instance, even feed their mates while copulating with them.[13] As far as anyone knows, courtship feeding is not performed by any other vertebrates, except for its occasional practice by humans.

While food can act as a sexual stimulant, its main use in the animal kingdom is in nourishing

16

the body and keeping animals alive and healthy. Because of its importance for survival, conflicts can develop within animal groups when food is scarce or when not every portion is equally palatable. In most cases the animal with the highest status or the greatest strength wins the conflict. Such is the case with our nearest relative, the chimpanzee, whose social group is dominated by an alpha male and his coalition partners. Members with higher status rule those with lower status, and when a female comes into estrus the alpha male has first choice in mating with her. Unlike the chimpanzee, the bonobo—an offshoot of chimpanzees—settles food and other conflicts with sex. Bonobos indulge in much genito-genital rubbing, and copulation lasts an average of thirteen seconds. So when situations arise that might lead to conflict, bonobos use sex to divert attention and settle the issue peacefully.

Humans, like bonobos, use sex for purposes other than procreation. And like humans, bonobos use rubbing and tongue-kissing as signals of readiness for more sexual activity.[14] It almost seems as if humans have picked up some of the bonobo genes!

Life has been well served by signals, signs, and symptoms, for they have been able to keep life going for three and a half billion years. So what brought symbolism into being? Why do humans need it, and how does it differ from signals, signs, and symptoms? These questions and how symbolism relates to the supernatural will be discussed in the coming chapters.

CHAPTER II

Creating and Reacting to Symbols and Symbolic Systems

Observations of Helen Keller

The difference between signals and symbols emerges quite pointedly when Helen Keller, who became blind and deaf at nineteen months of age, writes in her autobiography about how her teacher, Anne Mansfield Sullivan, exposed her to language by tapping into her hand. The following two episodes, which occurred when Helen Keller was almost seven years old, speak to this difference. In the first episode she writes:[1]

> The morning after my teacher came she led me into her room and gave me a doll. The little blind children at the Perkins Institution had sent it. When I had played with it a little while, Miss Sullivan slowly spelled into my hand the word "d-o-l-l." I was at once interested in this finger play and tried to imitate it. When I finally succeeded in making the letters correctly I was flushed with childish pleasure and pride. Running downstairs to my mother I held up my hand and made the letters for doll. I didn't know that I was spelling a

word or even that words existed. I was simply making my fingers go in monkey-like imitation. In the days that followed I learned to spell in this uncomprehending way a great many words, among them pin, hat, cup and a few verbs like sit, stand, and walk.

A few weeks later Helen wrote about the second episode:

She brought me my hat, and I knew I was going out into the sunshine. This thought, if a wordless sensation may be called a thought, made me hop and skip with pleasure. We walked down the path to the well-house, attracted by the fragrance of the honeysuckle with which it was covered. Someone was drawing water and my teacher placed my hand under the spout. As the cool stream gushed over my hand she spelled into the other the word water, first slowly, then rapidly. I stood still, my whole attention fixed upon the motion of her fingers. Suddenly, I felt a misty consciousness as of something forgotten—a thrill of returning thought; and somehow the mystery of language was revealed to me. I knew then that "w-a-t-e-r" meant the wonderful cool something that was flowing over my hand. That living word awakened my soul, gave it light, hope, joy, set it free!

One can sense how much more emotionally significant the second episode was than the first, even though both included the tapping of letters into her hand by her teacher. The tapping in the first episode seemed a game to Helen; a signal to imitate what the teacher was doing. Helen became

excited when she learned to follow the tapping
pattern, but the tapping itself had no further
significance. She felt the same excitement when
Miss Sullivan brought her hat to her—a signal that
she was about to be taken outside. In these cases,
Helen regarded the tapping and the hat as signals—
one prompted her to act, and the other alerted her
to what was coming. In the second episode, however,
the tapping represented an object, it symbolized
water. It didn't prompt her to act or alert her to
something coming. Instead, it made her contemplate
its meaning. This is the difference between a sign
or signal and a symbol. That a particular tapping
pattern could stand for something else—could be a
symbol—was such a significant realization that it
changed Helen's whole life. Her words to this
effect are so emotional that they can bring one to
tears: "That living word awakened my soul, gave it
light, hope, joy, set it free."

The Difference Between Signals and Symbols

The difference between signals or signs and symbols
is quite striking. It's the difference between
actually hearing a rattle while taking a walk and
hearing someone mention the word "rattlesnake" in
a conversation. The word is a symbol that represents
the snake: it can conjure up an image of a snake,
recall experiences you've had with rattlesnakes,
things you've learned about rattlesnakes, or other
thoughts or feelings about snakes. Hearing its
rattle, on the other hand, is a signal that alerts
you to danger and prompts you to act—you either
stop, make a wide path around the snake, or try
to get it to move away. Symbols have the property

of bringing something to your mind on which to contemplate or reflect, whereas signals, signs, and symptoms make you alert to something that is happening or about to happen. In essence, symbols are a call to reflection, while signals, signs, and symptoms are calls to action.

If someone speaks to you in a language you have never heard, it sounds like gibberish. If someone tapped into your hand using a manual alphabet or finger-spelling, you might wonder if they were getting fresh or playing a game. If you weren't familiar with American Sign Language and someone started making finger gestures in front of you, you might be impressed with their agility but you would have no idea that they were trying to communicate anything. Nevertheless, young children who are unfamiliar with spoken language, finger-spelling, or American Sign Language can catch on to these symbolic systems readily and can use them to communicate.

Blind people can be taught to read using Braille dot patterns; deaf people can learn to read lips; and people who are both blind and deaf can communicate in Morse code, using equipment that vibrates instead of clicks.

There seems to be no end to our ability to learn symbolic systems, for the human brain is genetically prepared to comprehend that a given sound, a given gesture, a given tap, or a given mark can represent something else, be it in the outside world or inside one's self. Topping off this marvelous ability is the talent of translating one language into another and one symbolic system into a different symbolic system. (A recent example is that of eight-year-old Wendy Vo, who has learned to speak eleven languages, including English, French, Vietnamese,

Hindi, Arabic and Russian.[2]) There are at least six thousand different languages spoken throughout the world.[3] We have even learned to program machines that can translate the symbols of one language into another. The language of mathematics, which uses numbers instead of words, is another example of how the human brain is programmed to develop symbolic systems that can be applied to the world we have inherited and inhabited.

Dreams and Symbols

If, as I have suggested, humans have been endowed by evolution with a symbolic brain, when and how does symbolic expression become active? We know that children can learn to use words at about eighteen months and can even make marks on a paper at that age to represent objects and family members. This was the age at which my own granddaughter made marks for each member of her family. But does the brain produce symbols before they can be consciously expressed via words or drawings?

What about dreaming? In dreams the brain produces symbols without conscious input, night after night without end. Dream researchers have shown that dreams occur during the rapid eye movement (REM) phase of sleep, and that when active brain waves are recorded on an electroencephalograph, the sleeper is dreaming. According to sleep experts, "It is now widely acknowledged that dreaming sleep and REM sleep are identical. The REM of the dreamer corresponds to the dreamer scanning the visual event of the dream scene."[4]

So, by figuring out when REM sleep first shows up in children, it can then be determined when dreaming starts. A research team undertook this kind of study believing that infants do not have REM sleep and therefore do not dream. Still, they wanted to know how brain waves during sleep change from the newborn to the infant to the toddler, so that they could find out when dreaming begins.[5] The study's startling discovery was that newborns not only engage in REM sleep, but they show an almost direct transition from wakefulness to REM sleep, unlike adults, for whom the first REM sleep occurs approximately fifty to seventy minutes after the onset of sleep. Moreover, REM sleep comprises a high proportion of total sleep in the first days of life and diminishes as maturation proceeds. The neonate spends fully a half of its total sleep time and one-third of its entire existence in this state. The authors conclude that infants dream a lot. While their dreams cannot consist of a succession of hallucinatory visual images, such as constitute normal adult sleep, they can consist of rudimentary hallucinations in other sensory modalities such as touch, warmth, wetness, and movement, since it is known that congenitally blind individuals have REM sleep and report dreaming.

For example, a study analyzing 372 dreams from fifteen blind adults revealed that those who had been blind since birth reported no visual imagery but a high percentage of taste, smell, and touch hallucinations. They also reported a high per-centage of locomotion/transportation dreams, which reflects the difficulty blind people face in traveling from place to place. Some congenitally blind individuals had dreams where "looking" and "seeing" seemed to be metaphorical in nature. A fifty-two-year-old woman dreamed that she and her husband (also blind) visited Thomas Jefferson at Monticello and reported that Jefferson took them to "see" plants in his garden. Likewise, a forty-six-year-old man dreamed that he went to a maternity hospital to "see" his first grandchild, "just like in real life," which was based on his recent experience of holding his grandchild. Many subjects reported strong sensory experiences in their dreams like feeling the warmth of the sun, the texture of a coat, the edge of a knife, vibrations, or the soft fur of a dog. They also experienced the smell of fire, tobacco, aftershave lotion, fresh air, food, and coffee. They noted the taste of a cigar, a cup of coffee, and an orange. In general, the imagery and sensations in the dreams of blind subjects were continuous with the senses they used in their waking lives.[6]

Symbolism Learning and Natural Selection

In light of the above studies, it seems that our symbolic brain starts its symbolic production right from birth, if not sooner. But it takes a while for children's brains to master the comprehension and translation of new symbolic systems, so the sounds of "ma," "pa," "him," "her," "no," and "yes" take more than a year to be understood as symbolic expressions. On the other hand, the body and brain respond to signals and symptoms from the body and the outside world all the time. A baby responds to these signals with crying, flailing, and cooing. Signals of hunger, thirst, pain, and bowel movements don't have to be learned; they are sensed from the beginning of life. Once symbolic language develops, however, children can express more directly what's bothering them—what they want to eat or drink, what scary things they dream about, and how they feel.

Symbolic expression can also act as a substitute for direct expression of emotions such as anger and hostility. For example, in his book on child development, Dr. Stanley Greenspan states, "A child who has not begun to express anger through ideas will not use that emotion during play and will resort to more concrete forms of expression when he is upset, such as hitting, biting, or having a tantrum." Greenspan goes on to trumpet a three-year-old child's ability to take a baby doll, pretend it's her sister, and express her anger at the doll, instead of dumping her baby sister out of her infant seat.[7]

While symbolic understanding and expression are evolutionary latecomers in the march of animal capabilities, they must have had survival and reproductive value from the beginning. The ability to substitute for the direct expression of anger and hostility, which could lead to retaliation and dire consequences, certainly aids survival. The ability of males and females to conceive strategies for obtaining sex would, more than likely, find a room in the house of natural selection. Planning ahead and substituting symbolic action for direct action seem to be two significant ways our symbolic brain helps us cope with life. Likewise, children can learn symbolically rather than through direct experience. For example, reading a book to a child about scuba diving, mountain climbing, firefighting, or skydiving allows the child to participate imaginatively in these activities without actually having to do them. Watching or being involved in a play or role-playing about divorce or ethnic rivalry allows participants to experience the conflicts, relationship issues, and social issues involved without going through the actual experiences. The ability of symbolic learning to teach us about the world and ourselves rests on its power to evoke the same emotions of awe, anxiety, pride, fear, shame, power, compassion, and empathy that the actual situations would produce.

Drawbacks of a Symbolic Brain

Evolution has endowed us humans with a symbolic brain with great potential for avoiding misguided behavior, learning without having to go through potentially trying experiences, and planning to achieve goals. What, if any, are the shortcomings of our symbolic brain? For one thing, we can use our imagination to scare the hell out of ourselves or other people. I recall teenagers scaring us smaller kids with tales of man-eating apes in the woods around our neighborhood, which we wouldn't enter unless they were with us. I was also totally convinced that if you swore on the Bible and were not truthful, God would kill you during the night. Misinformation can be transmitted and believed without actually having to experience something. Our symbolic brain thus opens us up to false beliefs, prejudice, and manipulation by others. False beliefs get tacked onto different physical appearances, and racial stereotypes develop. In his book on human evolution entitled *Ape Man*, Ron Caird asserts: "There are obvious differences between the people of the world. Some are black, some are white, some are yellow, and with these skin colors go a set of characteristic hair and facial features. For some reason humans like to endow these differences with great significance, to attach ideas of superiority to one appearance over another. This habit has led to great conflict, pain, and destruction. Racism is one of the most negative manifestations of the working of the human brain."[8]

Beliefs hold fast when they are surrounded by an emotional firewall. You don't need to experience or know the factual basis of your beliefs in order to maintain them. They might make you feel safer in a world of change, unpredictable events, challenges, and danger, and in the short run this could be helpful. But in the long run it could be harmful. Just look at the latest crisis in the US economic system, where an underlying belief in a free market without government regulation eventually proved untenable. This belief allowed corporations and their CEOs to rake in spectacular profits without considering the effect on the general public. Beliefs that are far outside the norm are considered paranoid or crazy. But there are still so-called normal people in the world who believe that the earth is flat that aliens from other planets roam among us, that the dead communicate with the living, and that Armageddon is just around the corner.

The Psychological Immune System and Our Symbolic Brain

Human achievement has been monumental, but so have human flaws. As stated earlier, natural selection smiled down on the human symbolic brain because of its ability to improve the chances for survival and reproduction. In my book *The Psychological Immune System*, I envision our symbolic brain as an important tool used extensively by our psychological immune system (Psy-IS) in its quest to protect, preserve, and enhance the life, property, and identity of ourselves and those we love and are bonded to.[9] The Psy-IS is programmed like the biological immune system to be ever on the alert for threats. The built-in or innate emotional response to a threat is rapid and directs us to avoid or destroy the threat. If other people are perceived as posing a threat, the reaction can be lethal—considering all our weapons—unless we can prevent or redirect it. Our symbolic brain can prevent a direct response by conceiving of alternatives and symbolic substitutes for our innate reaction. Hence, its protective nature.

Conversely, our symbolic brain can also conjure up ways to deal with people who are considered potential threats, even when the evidence against them is slim or nonexistent.

The killing of Jews who were suspected of purposely spreading bubonic plague around AD 1300 is one such example.

The internment of persons of Japanese ancestry on the West Coast during World War II is another. The invasion of Iraq because Saddam Hussein was suspected of having weapons of mass destruction and catering to Al Qaeda is a more recent example.

We pass on false beliefs by word of mouth, newspapers, magazines, radio, and television, and now the Internet. Younger kids believe older kids, older kids believe grown-ups, and grown-ups believe their leaders. It's the natural chain of a status hierarchy that is built into human nature. Reliance on dominance and status has been passed down the umbilical cord of life and can be seen in our closest relatives, the chimpanzees, who were studied closely for thirty years in Gombe, Tanzania, by Jane Goodall.[10]

Success in acquiring mates has also been part and parcel of the continuation of life. Many studies have shown that women who want to raise a family look for men who are willing to commit to a long-term relationship. Many men are willing to make this commitment but often have a competing plan, namely, to skip the commitment part and procreate with many women. The different goals of men and women were brought out in a three-day conference on mind, culture, and evolution. David Buss and Martie Haselton, two evolutionary psychologists, reported that evidence for the divergent mating goals of men and women can be found in their complaints. Women get most annoyed when men falsely promise commitment in order to get sex, while men get most annoyed when women falsely promise sex in order to get commitment.[11] Making a promise is one way of getting someone else to believe you—somewhat like a businessman making a guarantee—but when the belief gets dashed it can lead to hard feelings and the desire to get even.

Interaction Between Our Motivation and Our Symbolic Brain

The model for the psychological immune system is based on the fact that life depends upon protective mechanisms. This manifests itself in humans as the innate desire to survive, which means to protect, preserve, and enhance human life and physical well-being. There is also an innate desire to protect property and possessions. Consciousness of ourselves has extended this protective program to our sense of self and identity. These desires, with their emotional accompaniments, translate themselves into the motivation to protect, preserve, and enhance the life, possessions, and identity of ourselves and those we love and are bonded with. When we humans are motivated to accomplish something, our symbolic brains kick into gear and respond with ideas, visions, and plans that lead to programs and projects. This motivation didn't start with modern life but goes back to the beginning of human existence.

What programs and projects do these include? These are programs that maintain a cohesive family and society, secure food and water, neutralize or eliminate threats, protect against the elements, and train new members to handle the challenges faced by a social group. From hunting game and tending to family gardens we have developed the livestock and agricultural industries to provide our food. For protection against the elements have come the clothing and housing industries, along with heating and air conditioning. The creation of weapons has helped in securing food and eliminating threats, especially from human enemies. Our symbolic brain is always on call, and its initial creation of clubs and spears has led to the birth of atomic weapons. The motivation to create more lethal weapons will remain as long as fear remains. Likewise, evolution has given us a biological immune system with which to deal with the multitude of pathogens in our environment and we have helped it along, when it falls short, by developing the medical and pharmaceutical industries. In essence, the smallpox vaccine and the atomic bomb arose from the same motivation—namely, to protect, preserve, and enhance human life and physical well-being.

Also going way back to the beginning of humankind is the imperative to protect, preserve, and enhance property and possessions. This has its roots in the nature of our ancestors—including chimpanzees—to protect and defend their food sources and living spaces. When our ancestors learned to make stone tools millions of years ago, these were added to the possessions that needed protection. Acheulean stone tools—named for tools found at Saint-Acheul, France—were first made around 1.4 million years ago and continued to be made by our ancestor, *Homo erectus*, for a million years. They include hand axes, picks, flat-edged cleavers, and other carving instruments. They have been found in a region stretching from Africa, through most of Europe, the Near East, and India.[12] If various groups lived close enough to make contact with each other, they may have fought or bartered with each other for the stone quarries or the finished tools. This could have been the beginning of modern economics, with subsequent bartering for cattle, cowrie shells (the shells of mollusks), amber, grain, wampum (strings of beads made from clam shells), and metals.

Money and Banking to Guide Economics

According to Dr. Glen Davies, former professor of banking and finance at the University of Wales Institute of Science and Technology, banking originated in Babylonia around 3000 BC, when people used temples they trusted to store their valuables. Initially, deposits of grain were accepted; later, other goods including cattle, agricultural implements, and precious metals were also accepted. Eventually, metallic coins were used as a standard of value for trade. Military conquests, such as those of Alexander the Great, spread the use of coins, which became the most convenient means of payment. Coins remained the most important form of money right up to 1914, using gold as a standard. Because coins were the predominant form of payment, governments controlled minting. The development of modern banking and paper money broke the government monopoly of money creation and fostered the growth of modern economics. Nowadays, with credit cards and electronic transfers, coins are the very small change in a modern country's money supply, where abstract forms predominate. Dr. Davies contends that modern economies have come about, not as the result of dramatic inventions like the printing press, computer, or laser, but simply through gradual modifications in the use of money in carrying out its function as a unit of account in which debts and credits are calculated.[13] Economic experts and those in charge of economics have used their symbolic brains to change and modify the system so that it works on their behalf to make more money. The crash of the economic system in 2008 showed us how complex the interactions of banking had become. We have been exposed to terms and concepts like hedge funds, subprime and distressed loans, short-selling, frozen liquidity, toxic assets and toxic securities, backup capital, derivatives, and credit default swaps. When I listen, it makes me wonder where our symbolic brain power is leading us.

Keeping Our Sense of Self and Identity Safe

As stated earlier, evolution has endowed us with the gift of consciousness, which gave birth to our concept of self and our sense of identity. This allowed us to feel the warmth of camaraderie with those who share our cultural identity. Those groups who were able to maintain their cultural identity survived longer than those who did not. This is why natural selection looked favorably on a strong sense of individual and cultural identity. This conclusion is promoted by anthropologist Jack Weatherford in his book *Savages and Civilization*, which presents strong evidence that the development of self-awareness and identity was an evolutionary change that had survival value for our species.[14] However, as the model of the psychological immune system brings out, this change added another area, in addition to life and property, that needed protection. We humans alone have this challenge to wrestle with, as no other animal has a conceptual part of itself to protect that is just as important as its physical part. So we can't learn from our animal friends and ancestors how best to handle this challenge.

What have we done to protect, preserve, and enhance the sense of self and identity of ourselves and those we love and culturally identify with? It appears that we have developed three primary conceptual strategies with our symbolic brains.

The first of these follows, in principle, the hierarchical strategy of our closest relative, the chimpanzee. We depend, much as chimps do, on alpha males and their coalitions for leadership and on the maintenance of a social order—class distinctions—for the rest of the group. While we have usually relied on leadership passed down from generation to generation, as in dynasties of pharaohs or kings, new leadership has sometimes arisen through strong-arm tactics like the ones Fidel Castro used in Cuba, or through systems in which group members vote for their leaders, like the one the United States uses. With the strong-arm method, individuals who are low in the social order can rise to the top in a hurry if they have the military strength to do so; with the voting method, it may take centuries for low-ranking citizens to rise to the top, as the 2008 US election has shown. But in addition to the innate tendencies that chimps use to find their position in the social hierarchy, humans find their positions via their economic status, education, work skills, celebrity, and ability to impress others with their personality. Finding one's status in society, hanging on, and taking the opportunity to move up the ladder are methods that humans still use to protect, preserve, and enhance their sense of self and identity.

The second conceptual strategy humans have developed is that of embracing members of their own ethnic or cultural group (self-members) as worthy of our help and protection. This strategy depends on our ability to identify and deal with persons who do not belong (non-self members)—and who may pose a threat to the self-members. The impetus for this comes from the built-in survival program of the psychological immune system to detect threats to ourselves and our loved ones. We humans are always trying to detect who does and who doesn't fit into our group. This occurs throughout the world and leads to many a combative interaction between groups and nations. It can be seen on a non-threatening level in the intense rivalry between schools in their sporting teams, but it takes on a more ominous aspect in the rivalry between gangs. There is a need all over the world to be accepted, to feel special, to be respected, and to believe in oneself. Every parent would like to tell his or her child, "You can do anything you strive to do, and you can be anybody you want to be." If this belief sinks in, then parents have more faith in and worry less about their children's ability to protect, preserve, and enhance their sense of self and identity in this complicated and competitive world.

The third strategy for protecting and enhancing self and identity rests on the partially innate and partially learned regard for fairness and justice. Psychologist Frans B. M. de Waal is convinced that our sense of justice is an extension of that found in the chimpanzees, who display anger in response to perceived injustice. In his own words, "It is highly significant that violations of reciprocity or expected behavior elicit moralistic aggression among chimpanzees as among humans. In at least a few instances, nonhuman primates behave in ways that are readily recognizable as a root of the human anger in response to perceived injustice."[15] If one is around children, one can easily see their strong emotional reaction to a perception of unfairness or rule-breaking. "That's not fair, I was there first!" and "He's not playing by the rules. He's not being fair!" can frequently be heard. At age ten, I with several of my friends came upon a dead person lying on the ground with his throat cut behind a hardware store, where we all knew gambling took place. It didn't take long for us to conclude that this person was killed because he was caught cheating. The concept of fairness and justice was well entrenched in us children at this early age.

When humans feel disrespected or unfairly treated by the powers that be, as the original American colonists felt under England's rule, they eventually push back angrily and demand treatment that values their identity. Under the right political circumstances, these demands become embodied in the standards, codes, and values of a society and are incorporated into an individual's sense of self. In the United States we have the Bill of Rights, and for an idealized world we have the UN's Universal Declaration of Human Rights. However, as we can see by the controversy created by California's Proposition 8, which in 2008 limited marriage to heterosexual couples, there is still strong disagreement about what is fair and just. The courts will continue to have the challenge of figuring out when a situation, a controversy, or a law violates an individual's or a group's sense of justice and hence fails to protect or preserve their sense of self and identity.

The Importance of Our Belief System

It can be seen from the foregoing discussion that our symbolic brain responds to the emotional impact of different ideas, concepts, experiences, dreams, and social challenges, all of which shape our belief system and which, in turn, shapes our behavior. Helen Keller first believed that her teacher's tapping into her hand was a sort of game and responded accordingly. If you believe the rattle that you hear is that of a rattlesnake, you will react accordingly and take evasive action. If you believe, as Freud did, that dreams reveal your unconscious desires and feelings, you will pay special attention to them. False beliefs, such as Iraq was sheltering terrorists and hiding weapons of mass destruction, have profound effects on the actions we take. Now the Treasury Secretary believes that the $700 billion bailout of our failing economy will do the trick, but others are not so sure. Finally, there is an overriding belief among most people that fairness and justice will prevail over unfairness and injustice. How our beliefs affect our physical well-being, our psychological well-being, and our response to diseases has been an ongoing focus of biology, medicine, and psychology, and will be elaborated on in the coming chapters.

CHAPTER III

How Belief Affects Your Physical and Psychological Well-Being

A Prison Experiment: Reaction to Beliefs

Dr. Bernard Lown, a world-renowned cardiologist and Nobel Peace Prize recipient, reports a story in his book *The Lost Art of Healing* about a criminal in an Indian prison. Since he was condemned to death by hanging, the prison authorities allowed an experiment to be conducted by a Hindu physician, who, with the prisoner's consent, tapped into the prisoner's imagination. This is how Dr. Lown relates the story:[1]

> The doctor persuaded the prisoner to permit himself to be exsanguinated—bled to death—assuring him that death, though gradual, would be painless. The convict, on agreeing, was strapped to a bed and blindfolded. Vessels filled with water were hung at each of the four bedposts and set up to drip into basins on the floor. The skin on his four extremities was scratched, and the water began to drip into the containers, initially fast, then progressively slowing. By degrees the prisoner grew weaker,

a condition reinforced by the physician's intoning in a lower and lower voice. Finally the silence was absolute as the dripping of water ceased. Although the prisoner was a healthy young man, at the completion of the experiment, when the water flow stopped, he appeared to have fainted. On examination, however, he was found to be dead despite not having lost a single drop of blood.

This story illuminates the profound impact that a belief can have on one's life. Here the belief was absolute, as there was nothing that raised any doubts in the prisoner's mind. Because of our symbolic brain, as long as emotional impact is present, beliefs can be created without having to go through actual experiences. Children come to believe in the tooth fairy and ghosts, without having to encounter them in real life.

Dreaming provides another example. What takes place in your dream feels real, and your body reacts to the dream as if it were real. Your heart rate, blood pressure, muscle tension, and release of hormones are all affected by your dreams. People who sleepwalk are responding to the dream content as if it were reality. My son, when he was about three years old, got up out of bed and started walking into the kitchen, where I followed him. I didn't know he was sleepwalking at the time, so I asked him what he was doing. He answered that he had to use the "potty" and was about to urinate on the kitchen floor when I quickly diverted him to the bathroom. When he reached the bathroom he woke up and didn't remember going into the kitchen. Similarly, most teenage boys, if they are truthful, can tell you about "wet dreams" in which their sexual urges are imaginatively—and physically—expressed. In essence, one's reaction to beliefs is not always bound to reality. But reality-bound or not, beliefs leave their impact.

Dreaming Up False Beliefs

Psychotic delusions and hallucinations are like dreams, except they occur while the individual is awake in his or her own fantasy world. Elyn R. Saks, a professor of law at the University of Southern California, courageously provides vivid accounts of her delusions and hallucinations during psychotic episodes in her book *The Center Cannot Hold*. Here is a candid example of an episode she describes, which occurred after she had completed her first year at Yale Law School and was home for the summer.[2]

> And now here I was back home again, completely off antipsychotic meds and somewhat functional, although just barely on some days. Good days, bad days. More bad days. I went to the beach with my brother and sister-in-law, and the light and heat almost made me cower. In minutes, I was convinced that everyone there had come to the beach to ambush me—they thought I was evil, that I had killed many people. I was certain that if I moved suddenly, they'd leap up and kill me. I sat stiff as a board on my towel near the water, silently begging not to be noticed. I wished I had brought a gun with me to protect myself in case I was attacked.

Despite the fact that Saks knew where she was and who she was with, her belief system was not connected to the reality of the situation but rather to the anxiety that arose from her imagined perception of imminent threats. Still, a part of her remained aware that her beliefs were not always based on reality, and thus she had a constant battle going on inside her head between her psychotic beliefs and her sense of reality. This is the way Professor Saks describes it:

> The constant effort to keep reality on one side and delusions on the other was exhausting, and I often felt beaten down, knowing that the schizophrenia diagnosis had ended any hope I'd had of a miracle cure or a miracle fix. I disappointed my family; I'd shamed them. I wondered aloud if I would ever amount to anything. "Maybe it's too late," I said. "Maybe I need to be realistic about my life."

That she was eventually able to come to grips with her struggle for reality is a testament to her perseverance and her strength to bounce back again and again. In the end she learned to believe in herself and stay in control.

Beliefs Affect the Body

As the story about the prisoner dramatically shows, beliefs can have a profound effect on an individual's physical well-being. No matter the source of the beliefs—whether from dreams, stories told to children, or psychotic delusions—they all produce a physiological impact on the body by way of the emotions they generate. As previously explained, your psychological immune system is programmed to detect and identify threats without ceasing. This means that events are always being evaluated to differentiate what is safe from what is dangerous. Your brain has the task of forming beliefs about the degree of danger present and, if necessary, of preparing you to act. Therefore evolution has made sure that your beliefs are connected to the physiological processes of your body—by way of your emotions—to ensure your survival. Thus your body is ready to respond, no matter whether your beliefs are realistic or fanciful. The fields of medicine and psychology are both keenly interested in, and have done much research about, how your beliefs interact with and affect your physical and psychological well-being.

The Placebo Effect

An important area of interest is the placebo effect or the placebo response, which pharmaceutical companies have to take into account when testing drugs on human subjects. If they fail to rule out this effect, they can never be sure whether the effect of the drug they are testing is due to its chemical action or to the patient's belief about the drug's effect. The power of belief is the driving factor in the placebo effect, and it can kindle both positive and negative consequences.

Dr. Andrew Weil, director of the program in integrative medicine at the University of Arizona, provides an example of the negative consequences of the placebo effect in his book *Spontaneous Healing*.[3] He describes a patient with advanced prostate cancer who was offered hormone treatment by his urologist as "the only treatment worth doing." Since the patient was a heavy smoker, he asked his doctor if it would be helpful to stop smoking. He told Dr. Weil that his urologist answered, "At this point why bother?" He took this answer to mean that he would die soon. Weil states that this created terror in the patient, "a terror that paralyzed him and prevented him from making constructive efforts for his own survival and well-being."

Weil equates the urologist's statement to that of a witch doctor or shaman putting a curse on a person. He goes on to say that doctors in our culture are invested with the same power that was projected onto shamans and priests during the Middle Ages and that "so-called voodoo death—medical hexing—is the ultimate example of a negative placebo response."

For the positive consequences of the placebo effect, Dr. Weil refers to Lourdes, France, where sick and disabled people go to the "healing baths" and many miraculous cures are claimed. He states that each case of a miraculous cure is reviewed by three panels of physicians, and that since 1947 seventy-five cases have been reviewed and accepted as having documented illnesses with established diagnoses. Of the seventy-five cases accepted, about twenty-seven "cures" were considered inexplicable. The Catholic Church pronounced seventeen of the cases to be miracles.

In his book *The Biology of Mind*, M. Deric Bownds, emeritus professor of molecular biology and zoology at the University of Wisconsin, reinforces the idea of "miracle cures" when he writes, "Some quite remarkable cases of mood- or belief-caused remission of the symptoms of illnesses such as cancer, arthritis, asthma, and acute depression have been documented. In many of these cases, a sham treatment called a placebo (Latin for 'I shall please') is administered; it is believed by the patient to be an effective drug or therapy." He goes on to say that "expectancy—what the brain is telling the body it expects to happen—has a powerful effect on the actual outcome. The mind-body connection reaches down to the intricate details of our immune system biochemistry."[4]

Knowledge of the placebo effect goes back a long way, at least to the Second World War. It was noticed by Lt-Col. Henry Beecher of the US Army Medical Corps, who was treating soldiers wounded in combat. He found that if soldiers in great pain were given a placebo—a substance with no pain-killing properties—about 35 percent reported marked relief from pain. This led him to the opinion that this effect was similar to the effect of suggestion during hypnosis.[5] In fact there is a similarity between the placebo effect and hypnosis, as both depend on a high regard for the practitioner and a belief that what is being offered has merit. In addition, there are variations in the degree to which subjects respond to both hypnosis and the placebo effect. Some individuals are dramatically affected—the high responders—and some show very little effect—the low responders. Most people fall in between. In his book *Anatomy of an Illness*, Norman Cousins quotes Dr. Albert Schweitzer—a prominent missionary doctor to Africa who received the Nobel Peace Prize—in explaining the placebo effect.

Schweitzer states, "Each patient carries his own doctor inside him. They come to us not knowing that truth. We are at our best when we give the doctor who resides within each person a chance to work." So Norman Cousins concludes that "the placebo is the doctor who resides within."[6]

Physical Underpinnings of the Placebo Effect

Some recent studies using brain-imaging positron emission tomography (PET) scans and brain chemistry analysis have shed light on which parts of the brain are activated during the placebo effect and what chemical responses, if any, are taking place. A study at the University of Michigan that focused on pain relief found that the brain's own pain-fighting chemicals, called endorphins (self-manufactured opioids) are produced. These chemicals bind to brain cell receptors and block the transmission of pain signals from one nerve cell to the next. This is the same method used by pain-killing drugs such as heroin, morphine, methadone, and anaesthetics.[7]

In Parkinson's disease, a chronic nervous system disease characterized by tremor and muscle weakness, about 50 percent of the patients show a positive placebo response. The biochemical changes underlying the placebo response seem to depend on the activation of dopamine, a neurotransmitter that improves mood, within different areas of the brain. As well as improvements in Parkinson's disease, the placebo response can also help during depressive episodes. In this case, the effect comes from mediating brain activity in the same way as antidepressive drugs, such as selective serotonin reuptake inhibitors (SSRIs). These drugs prevent the loss of serotonin at the synapse, a neurochemical which helps maintain a positive mood. The placebo response seems to follow a similar path.[8]

Thus it appears that beliefs about the benefits of medication evoke emotional responses that trigger biochemical reactions that actually benefit the patient. This is the positive placebo effect or response. Is the same also true of the negative placebo effects cited by Dr. Weil in the above section? Certainly, strong emotional reactions are evoked when people are told that they are living on borrowed time or that the angel of death is shadowing them. The belief that one is near death can produce sleepless nights and stressful days. As Dr. Lown remarks in *The Lost Art of Healing*, "Cardiologists have learned that psychological stresses can influence the most intimate aspects of heart function." He mentions disrupted heart rhythms, heart attacks, and sudden cardiac arrest.[9]

Like the positive placebo effect, the negative placebo effect, also called "the nacebo effect," has been studied by scientists hoping to uncover its underlying neurochemical activity. Research has shown that the nacebo effect is the result of a deactivation of the same systems that underlie the positive placebo effect—namely, the systems that produce dopamine and enhance the release of opioids (endorphins). The areas of the brain that are involved with these effects form part of the circuit usually activated when rewards or goal-directed behaviors are involved.[10] However, it must be recognized that in addition to the activation or deactivation of brain circuits, beliefs that stir up anxiety and prompt the nacebo effect can also produce feelings of stress that impact the brain and body.

Causes and Effects of Stress

Dr. Lown made reference to the effect of stress on heart functioning, but it is also known that prolonged stress can increase the risk of or worsen many diseases, such as hypertension, atherosclerosis, insulin-resistant diabetes, reproductive impairments, and mental disorders. Protracted stress suppresses the biological immune system and this opens individuals up to diseases that would otherwise not have taken hold.[11] In the same way, prolonged stress can have detrimental effects on the ability of your psychological immune system to protect, preserve, or enhance your life, property, and sense of self.[12] In our fast-paced society and with the pressure of time commitments we all face, who hasn't gotten stressed out by life?

Pressures at school, at work, at home, and on the streets—like being stuck in traffic—leave their mark. Some situations that have created stress for me as well as for my wife are my mother's nine-year battle with cancer; my upbringing without a father; hierarchy struggles with my peers; final exams at school; our son's problems with a bully at school; our daughter's "vanishing" on a bus while visiting a girlfriend in Los Angeles; getting lost while hiking in a national forest, and worrying about our dogs as they aged and developed physical problems for which there were no answers—to name just a few.

The ten greatest stressors, according to Richard Rahe, a leading stress researcher, are as follows: (1) death of a spouse, child, or other family member; (2) a major change in the health or behavior of a family member; (3) being fired, laid off, or demoted at work; (4) getting pregnant; (5) having a miscarriage or getting an abortion; (6) getting a divorce; (7) having a relative move in with you; (8) experiencing decreased income; (9) being held in jail; and (10) foreclosure on a mortgage or loan.[13]

The Body's Reaction to Stress

Dr. Hans Selye, a pioneer in stress research who was professor and director of the Institute of Experimental Medicine and Surgery at the University of Montreal, provides a thorough and insightful look at stress in his book *Stress Without Distress*.[14] Right from the start he impresses upon us that stress is everywhere in life and that "complete freedom from stress is death." The body reacts to stressful events with a biological stress syndrome or a general adaptation syndrome, which takes place in three stages: 1) the alarm reaction; 2) the stage of resistance; and 3) the stage of exhaustion. The last stage comes about after long continued exposure to the same stressor without sufficient relief. It follows that if one can learn to adjust to life's stresses—like overcoming frustrations—one can avoid reaching the stage of exhaustion.

Robert Sapolsky, a professor of biological science and neurology at Stanford University and an expert on stress, states that the body's response to stressful situations is the release of stress hormones that are "brilliantly adapted" to help one survive an unexpected threat to life or physical well-being. "You mobilize energy in your thigh muscles, you increase your blood pressure and you turn off everything that's not essential to surviving, such as digestion, growth, and reproduction." And: "You think more clearly and certain aspects of learning and memory are enhanced."

The release of adrenaline (epinephrine) and glucocorticoids (cortisol) from the adrenal glands prompts the above responses. However, these same hormones are released even in stressful non-life-threatening situations, like threats to your reputation or public image, or imagined threats that can occur during mental illness. If the stressors are chronic, as job-related, family-related, or imagined ones tend to be, then serious consequences can result, including diabetes, high blood pressure, gastrointestinal disorders, and greater susceptibility to disease. In children the release of glucocorticoids can suppress the secretion of normal growth hormones, and this can result in a syndrome called stress dwarfism.

Sapolsky sums up his stress research as follows: "We're about 70 years into thinking that sustained stress can do bad things to your health. The biggest challenge in the next 70 years is figuring out why some of us are so much more vulnerable than others." He recommends that people do whatever they can to reduce stress in their daily lives, by using stress management, changing their priorities, or going into therapy.[15]

Stress Management

From all the studies described above, it seems there's agreement that short-term stress can be beneficial but long-term stress can be harmful. It follows that if the effects of stress can be stopped after a relatively short period, the detrimental effects can be avoided and the beneficial effects savored. The question, of course, is how do you stop feeling stressed once you are exposed to stressful events?

Looking at all the things I listed that stressed me out, the best remedy was to let myself imagine the possible outcomes of each stressful situation, undertake a search of the options available to me, and finally make a decision about which option to choose. My personal experience and my professional observation of clients I have had in therapy lead me to believe that stressful situations create intense emotions that push your symbolic brain to imagine multitudes of paths or options that might be used to help you. If there are other people on whom you can bounce off your emotions and ideas, this is to your benefit. That's why peer and group interaction can be helpful in all kinds of stressful situations, such as dealing with the death of a loved one, learning to live with cancer, staying sober or drug-free, having to deal with highly charged family situations, or handling emotional abuse. I ran many, many groups for abusive families and their abused children, and I had the privilege of seeing the healing effects of peer and group interaction.

Stress and Social Support

Research on stress management backs up many of these same points. Numerous studies show, for example, that social support can decrease the output of stress hormones during traumatic situations. This seems to be true for other primates as well as for human beings, and it indicates that natural selection has chosen this interaction as beneficial for survival. Dr. David Spiegel, director of the Psychosocial Treatment Laboratory at the Stanford University School of Medicine, cites some of these studies in his article for the book *Mind Body Medicine*.

A study done on squirrel monkeys by psychologist Seymour Levine at Stanford University showed that the output of the stress hormone cortisol was cut in half when the stressed monkey had another monkey as company and was totally curtailed when the stressed monkey had five companions. Spiegel also cites his own study in which eighty-six women with breast cancer were randomly divided into two groups; one group was assigned to support groups with standard medical treatment while the other group was given standard medical treatment without the support groups. These are the results in his own words: "The most striking finding of our study was the one that only became apparent a decade after the groups had ended. We found that those in the support groups had lived an average of eighteen months longer than those in the control sample. Considering their stage of cancer when the study began, that added year and a half represented a virtual doubling of survival from the time they entered our study."[16]

Stress and the Sense of Control

When my sixteen-year-old daughter went by bus to visit her girlfriend in Los Angeles—about a one-hour trip—and didn't call to inform us of her arrival and her girlfriend hadn't heard from her after two and a half hours, I felt fearful and stressful. I got in touch with the LA Police Department but when they tried to transfer me to their downtown division, which covers the bus terminal, the connection got dropped every time they put me on hold. After I had been disconnected three times, my stress level went through the roof. Finally, after three hours my daughter called and informed me that she was fearful if getting off the bus at her designated stop because of the neighborhood and rode the bus to the end of its run and then called her friend to pick her up. What a relief! When I think back to that event, what comes through clearly is the lack of control I felt. There was nothing I could do but wait and sweat it out. I felt helpless!

Studies show, in fact, that the feeling of no control or helplessness plays a significant part in creating stress. Over time, feeling helpless can lead to depression. One of the leading authorities in this area is Dr. Martin Seligman, professor of psychology at the University of Pennsylvania and director of the Positive Psychology Network. He worked with two groups of dogs who, in the first part of his experiment, were given low-level electric shocks. One group could escape from the shocks by pressing on a lever; the second group couldn't escape no matter what they tried. In the second part of the experiment he placed both groups of dogs in a box from which they could escape the electric shocks by jumping over a low partition. The group that had been able to escape the shocks the first time rapidly learned to jump over the partition. But most of the dogs in the second group, which had been unable to escape the shocks in the first part of the experiment, simply lay down, absorbed the shocks, and whined. They never tried to jump over the partition. Seligman labeled this behavior "learned helplessness."[17]

This label has also been applied to humans who feel they have no control and who act helpless when they encounter stressful events. Seligman explains that although a group of people may experience the same or similar negative events, how each person interprets the event affects the likelihood of acquiring learned helplessness and subsequent depression. It appears that when a person encounters a trying situation, his response seems to depend upon whether he believes he has some control over the situation and whether he has faith in his own abilities and believes that things will get better in the future.[18]

The belief that one is unable to change things or that things are always beyond one's control is characteristic of a pessimistic outlook. The development of Positive Psychology, of which Seligman is a founder, attempts to undo the pessimistic outlook by using a common human skill called disputing. For example, if you do your job well and someone falsely accuses you of doing a poor job, you will dispute him and gather evidence to prove your point. Positive Psychology teaches individuals to dispute the negative thoughts that keep coming up about themselves and to develop "learned optimism." In Seligman's own words, "So in 'learned optimism' training programs, we teach both children and adults to recognize their own catastrophic thinking and become skilled disputers."[19] In essence, stress is reduced by learning how to control one's negative thinking.

How about being down on one's luck—for example, in the case of gamblers? What do gamblers do? According to sociologist James Henslin, who studied a group of crapshooters, they tap into their symbolic brains and come up with strategies and beliefs that border on the magical. This provides them with a sense of personal control over the randomness of probability. Here are some of the strategies and beliefs reported to Henslin: (1) hard throws produce large numbers, while soft throws produce low numbers; (2) talk to the dice and tell them what you want; talk to them when you shoot; (3) command the dice to roll the point you're after, such as "Six it!"; (4) be confident—it imparts success and control to the shooter, whereas to "get shook" is to lose confidence, to be deprived of your control and the ability to make your point; (5) bet "odd money," for example, a dollar and a penny or the exact amount of change in your opponent's pocket; (6) personal relationships affect the outcome of the game: a player known as Preacher won seven straight passes, which was attributed to his good relationship with God; "He reads the Good Book. Yessir! He's bettin' through the Book." Henslin refers to these beliefs as "rational irrationality."[20]

The Challenge of Sorting Out Beliefs

Evolution has provided you with a symbolic brain that through your experience, tries to make sense of the world by creating models, concepts, formulations, and opinions about how things function—especially how humans function. These concepts and models underlie your beliefs about the world, yourself, and your place in the world. What you believe affects your physical and psychological health through the emotional impact that your beliefs create, as has been shown by the studies and personal examples provided. False, unfounded, or questionable beliefs can have the same profound effect on your physical and psychological well-being as do well-founded and well-grounded beliefs. The placebo, nacebo, and stress effects are primary examples of the impact your beliefs have on your brain and on your nervous, endocrine, and immune systems. Natural selection has determined that your survival is aided by connecting your beliefs to your life, physical well-being, and sense of self.

But with your symbolic brain ready to create and accept imaginary or delusional beliefs, as well as realistic ones, you are up against trying to fit all sorts of myths, legends, superstitions, and magical beliefs into your life, and attempting to determine what is real and what is fantasy.

As the principles of the psychological immune system predict, the greater the threat confronting you, the greater the emotional reaction and the greater the tendency for you to come up with a fast, powerful response to reduce or eliminate the threat. But emotion can overwhelm your good judgment and your symbolic brain can come up with beliefs and plans that rest more on your fears and wishes than on reality. In this day and age, because of the overwhelming amount of information you are exposed to, sorting out real from unreal threats can be a difficult challenge, as can sorting out myths from reality. For example, some myths on the web that many people believe are as follows: drinking cold water after meals will lead to cancer; the medical industry is withholding from the public a cure for cancer in order to increase its profits; Chihuahuas can cure asthma in children by sleeping on them; and cats can suck the breath out of babies.

Despite all the scientific evidence available, a large percentage of the American population—and probably the world population—still believe in the supernatural. This is the subject of the next chapters, which will try to provide an understanding of why supernatural beliefs have persisted for centuries and continue to be widespread in the twenty-first century.

CHAPTER IV

Faith, Supernatural Beliefs, and Their Impact on Human Well-Being

Living with the Reindeer in Siberia

> The fire is the foundation of life. We feed, we warm ourselves, we're nourished with its help. Granny explained in a serious tone. And it protects us. Evil Spirits come out at night, don't they? So before they appear you should build up the fire, you know, keep it burning, keep it burning!! The fire should stay on all night to keep the spirits away.

This is how Granny, one of the elders of the Eveny people, explained the significance of fire to anthropologist Piers Vitebsky, who lived among and studied these people for nearly twenty years. The Eveny, who live and herd reindeer in the Verkhoyansk mountain range in northeast Siberia, where tempertures can plunge to -96 degrees Fahrenheit, are a hardy group of people, to say the least, and have to contend with issues of survival in a hostile environment every day of their lives.

In his book *The Reindeer People: Living with Animals and Spirits in Siberia,* Vitebsky, head of Anthropology and Russian Northern Studies at the Scott Polar Research Insitute at the University of Cambridge, tells the story of the Eveny partnership with the reindeer they have domesticated and on whom they depend for their survival.[1] The ninety active male herders, who are supported by their wives and other family members, are divided into thirteen brigades. They look after about 20,000 reindeer in northeast Siberia and have to follow the animals' migration within a 4,300-square-mile area. They have trained reindeer on which to ride and reindeer to pull sleds loaded with supplies. They have to be on constant guard against wolves, on constant alert for reindeer that stray, capable of fixing wounded reindeer hooves, rugged enough to handle all kinds of weather, able to set up and dismantle their tents on a daily basis, and knowledgeable about which routes through the mountains are passable and which are not. In short, they have to be and stay reality-oriented because their survival and that of their herds depend on it. And yet they believe in spirits that inhabit the rocks, trees, animals, fire, and everything they come in contact with.

It is not hard to understand what Granny had to say about fire, since fire can be considered one of the foundations of life. It provides warmth and heat for cooking and can be a source of protection. It can keep away predators who may be conceptualized as "the evil spirits" she warns about. So Granny's remarks do not seem too abnormal.

On the other hand, the Eveny ascribe magical properties to fire such as the ability to forewarn them of future events. It lets them know when a guest is coming, if a hunter will be successful, and when someone is going to die. The Eveny can ask the fire where their lost reindeer are by throwing a shoulder bone in the fire and reading the answer from cracks that develop in the bone. They seem to believe they can converse with the fire and that it understands what is being said, and that the fire has supernatural powers to see into the future. Its answers come in the form of sounds the fire makes or the cracks it makes in the bones. In essence, the fire is used as an instrument of divination. This seems to be the same role that psychics play in today's cities.

In addition to fire, in former times the Eveny put their faith in shamans, whom they believed could cure illnesses, see into the future, manipulate the weather, identify and fight evil spirits, protect herders and reindeer from harm, and even return from the dead as reincarnated members of a family. The Soviet Union's policy, however, was to rid these "backward people" of their reliance on shamans by imprisoning or killing individuals identified as shamans. Today there are no openly identified shamans among the Eveny people, and post-Soviet Russia has not changed this policy. Nevertheless, many Eveny still believe that certain members of their families have shamanic powers and may be reincarnated shamans. They're not about to openly display their powers and defy the state, but the concept of supernatural powers remains and embodies the Evenys' reverence for and appreciation of nature and the role it plays in their lives.

While the state may see shamans or others as threats to its powers and place restrictions on what its citizens can openly express, it cannot control the emotions and beliefs that come into peoples' consciousness. The Evenys' reverence for nature has helped keep their imagination active and has been a motivating force in maintaining their supernatural beliefs, along with their reality orientation about everyday survival tactics. Below are some factors that have helped stimulate and sustain supernatural beliefs.

Wishing for versus Believing in Supernatural Powers

What state of wonderment would fill you if you realized you were able to see into the future, manipulate the weather, cure illnesses, see and fight evil spirits, protect your family from harm, and return from the dead? The wish for such powers certainly occurs, but it's a lot different if one not only wishes for such powers but believes they can be attained. One may feel that he or she does not have the ability to develop these supernatural powers, but may yet believe that others can. If this is the case, then the next step would be to align oneself with such individuals. These powerful people would then become godlike, and one would only need to follow their pronouncements in order to benefit from them.

In fact, my book *The Psychological Immune System* spells out the human need for leadership that arises from the evolutionary path of our ancestors and other primates.[2] When we humans are faced with difficult situations, challenges, dangers, or life-changing opportunities, our symbolic brains go into overdrive and come up with imaginative ideas that may or may not be practical or realistic. If we're in doubt, we usually turn to experts or leaders who we feel can help us make the right decision. But if the experts and leaders are in doubt, to whom do they turn? Many turn to a "higher power" for wisdom and help. People seem to have an underlying faith that they can find answers to difficult problems if they keep going up the hierarchical ladder, even if it includes imaginary resources.

Human history may, in fact, be on the side of wishing for the impossible and then attaining it. Early man wished he could fly like a bird, and probably imagined being able to do so. Now we can fly in airplanes much faster than any bird. Humans wished to be able to go underwater and swim like fishes. Now we have scuba gear and submarines that have made these wishes come true. How many humans once looked at the moon and wondered what it would be like to visit it? Now that too has been done. Who has not wished for a medical miracle when his body parts have become defective or worn out? Now we have heart, lung, and kidney transplants as well as hip and knee replacements and we can even envision the transplantation of brains. There seems to be no end to human imagination and creativity. In fact, some theoretical physicists and astronomers talk about going through black holes and coming out into new universes. Is it any wonder that so many people continue to believe in spirits, ghosts, clairvoyance, and reincarnation?

This is what MIT professor Steven Pinker, one of the world's leading psychologists, states about supernatural beliefs in his book *How the Mind Works*.[3]

In culture after culture, people believe that the soul lives on after death, that rituals can change the physical world and divine the truth, and that illness and misfortune are caused and alleviated by spirits, ghosts, saints, fairies, angels, demons, cherubim, djinns, devils, and gods. According to polls, more than a quarter of today's Americans believe in witches, almost half believe in ghosts, half believe in the devil, half believe that the book of Genesis is literally true, sixty-nine percent believe in angels, eighty-seven percent believe that Jesus was raised from the dead, and ninety-six percent believe in a God or universal spirit.

Pinker seems to conclude, much like my thesis about our symbolic brain, that the structure of the human brain leads us to conjecture about everything, even if doing so leads to fictitious beliefs. Here is his concluding remark: "Our bafflement at the mysteries of the ages may have been the price we paid for a combinational mind that opened up a world of words and sentences, of theories and equations, of poems and melodies, of jokes and stories, the very things that make a mind worth having."

Symbols for Our Emotions and Feelings

In Chapter II, I related the story of Helen Keller's realization that a certain tapping pattern represented the water that was flowing over her hand, and how this realization changed her life. How would her teacher, Mary Sullivan, have been able to teach Helen that the tapping pattern of the word "awe" represented a certain emotion inside of Helen? She would have had to explain how awe comes about when experiencing some spectacular event or sensation, in the hope that Helen had perceived or felt this emotion herself.

Assuming we have all felt awe, and assuming we all speak the same language, then we can denote the emotion by a word-symbol and the experiences that brought this emotion about by more word-symbols. But what if you were in a foreign land and didn't speak the same language? How would you specify the emotion of awe without resorting to a translator? You could make facial expressions and hand gestures, draw pictures, or look at magazine pictures that convey an emotion of awe; you could take pictures of something awe-inspiring and show it to the person you are communicating with; or you could even show a video of someone climbing a mountain or surfing a fifty-foot wave or a falcon diving from a cliff to catch its prey. In effect you would be using representational images to depict the emotion.

Isn't it possible that myths, legends, rituals, and magical activities have been used to represent intense feelings and emotions that words alone cannot adequately represent? As an example, Joseph Campbell, in his book *The Power of Myth*, writes about what he believes the snake or serpent (which sheds its skin) symbolizes or represents. This is what he says: "The serpent represents immortal energy and consciousness engaged in the field of time, constantly throwing off death and being born again. There is something tremendously terrifying about life when you look at it that way. And so the serpent carries in itself the sense of both the fascination and the terror of life."[4] If such symbols are passed down from generation to generation and stories are created about the symbols, then we have the birth of myths and legends.

The Need for Power, Control and Spirituality

The Eveny use of fire to see into the future and find lost members of their herd; their reliance on shamans to control the weather, cure illness, and protect the community; their performance of rituals to change the physical world and divine the truth; and the widespread belief in angels and God—all represent their need for power and control to ensure their survival.

In addition, the awe-inspiring events we have encountered in our brief stay on earth, which create wonder, amazement, bewilderment, and astonishment, have triggered in us the passion to pay homage to something greater than ourselves—something we call "spirituality." Even astronomers who rely on Einstein's equations to explain the astronomical events they see must be amazed and spellbound when they observe two giant galaxies, each containing billions of stars, crashing into each other and realize that this event happened thousands of light-years ago! When I look at pictures of giant galaxies crashing into each other, it certainly amazes me. This is even more startling—from my perspective—than seeing surfers riding fifty-foot waves in Hawaii!

Supernatural Beliefs for Protecting Life

By being connected to and believing in supernatural forces, one can attain and maintain a feeling of power and control over the unknown, the dangers that lurk in the shadows, and the unpredictable situations that could arise at a moment's notice. This certainly provides comfort and reduces one's fears and anxieties. It also allows the sense that one is protecting, preserving, and enhancing the life and physical well-being of oneself and one's loved ones. Jacob Pandian, professor of anthropology at California State University, Fullerton, seems to feel that, indeed, this is the case. He writes,

> Historically humans have created beliefs and practices associated with supernatural beings and supernatural powers, and these beliefs and practices have been used to construct sacred self and group identities and to formulate models or narratives of coherence and meaning to cope with feelings of helplessness, encounters with suffering and injustice, realities of uncertainty, and fear and anxiety associated with sickness and death.[5]

So Pandian implies that supernatural forces and supernatural beliefs have been created as coping mechanisms to deal with adversity. He concludes that "this process of creating and maintaining the supernatural world will continue." In essence, this is a process of using symbolic creations to deal with our feelings of powerlessness and lack of control over the world. Our symbolic brain is well suited for producing symbolic creations.

Supernatural Beliefs for Enhancing Identity

Pandian's theorizing that supernatural beliefs and practices are used to "construct sacred self and group identities" resonates with a principle of the psychological immune system that says humans innately try to protect, preserve, and enhance the sense of self and identity of themselves and others whom they love. For example, the belief that one belongs to a group with superior powers or a group chosen by God is certainly a way of enhancing one's sense of self and identity. Consciousness of self and of man's unique creative talents is instrumental in fostering an egocentric outlook in most humans. It helps create the conviction that we are more important than all other animals; it perpetuates the belief that humans have a special place in the universe; and it prompts humans to rise above dealing only with physical and earthly matters. Thus, humans typically develop an inclination and motivation to deal with spiritual matters.

This can readily lead to the ideas of souls, spirits, angels, and other supernatural phenomena, which our symbolic brain is only too eager to produce. In fact, some observers believe that our attraction to spiritual matters has been genetically programmed into the human brain.

Dean Hamer's book *The God Gene: How Faith Is Hardwired into Our Genes* advances this belief. Hamer has pretty impressive credentials. He is a geneticist and director of the Gene Structure and Regulation Unit at the United States National Cancer Institute. His book is based on DNA analysis of more than a thousand people of different ages and backgrounds who were rated as to their spirituality on the "self-transcendence scale" created by psychiatrist Robert Cloninger of Washington University. Persons with high scores on this scale were found to have a slightly different version of a gene labeled VMAT2 (a monoamine transporter gene involved with the production of serotonin and dopamine), which Hamer designated as the "God gene."

This is how Hamer explains what he means by faith being hardwired into our genes and the idea of the God gene.[6]

In *The God Gene*, I propose that spirituality has a biological mechanism akin to birdsong, albeit a far more complex and nuanced one: that we have a genetic predisposition for spiritual belief that is expressed in response to and shaped by personal experience and the cultural environment. These genes, I argue, act by influencing the brain's capability for various types and forms of consciousness, which become the basis for spiritual experiences.

The term "God gene" is, in fact, a gross over-simplification of the theory. There are probably many different genes involved, rather than one. And environmental influences are just as impor-tant as genetics. Finally, spirituality in its broader meaning is about more than belief in a particular God. Some of the most spiritual people I've interviewed and discuss don't believe in a deity at all. Nevertheless, I felt it was a useful abbreviation of the overall concept.

Further evidence that spirituality is a natural part of our brain comes from the experience of neuroanatomist Jill Bolte Taylor, who suffered a massive stroke in 1996 at the age of thirty-seven and lived to tell about it in her book *My Stroke of Insight: A Brain Scientist's Personal Journey*.[7] The stroke was in the left hemisphere of her brain and left her unable to walk, talk, read, write, or recall any part of her life. In her own words, "I essentially became an infant in a woman's body."

After brain surgery to remove the hemorrhage that had accumulated in her brain, Taylor went to live with her mother, who took care of her as if she were an infant. It took eight years for Taylor to fully recover and resume her career at the

Indiana School of Medicine, and she took on the added role of spokesperson for the Harvard Brain Tissue Resource Center.

Taylor's book describes her thoughts and feelings during and after her stroke and how the loss of her left hemisphere was both frightening and emotionally freeing as she discovered the mystery of her right hemisphere—which became her "stroke of insight." She maintains that she became free from the left brain's competitive mode of thinking and acting, which she says often becomes aggressive and argumentative. She found that her right hemisphere connected her to a feeling of deep inner peace and opened her up to a deeper spiritual world, which she considers to be built into the right hemisphere. Here are some of the phrases she uses to describe her feelings: "My earthly body dissolved and I melted into the universe. My consciousness soared into an all-knowingness, a 'being at one' with the universe, if you will."

It is interesting to note that the self-transcendence scale used by Dean Hamer to measure spirituality has as one of its components the intensity with which an individual feels connected to a larger universe. So it sounds like Jill Bolte Taylor and Dean Hamer are riding on the same wavelength of spirituality.

Reasons Developed for Supernatural Beliefs

In the preceding sections of this and the previous chapter I have included several reasons for the creation and use of supernatural beliefs. (1) Among the Eveny in Siberia, supernatural beliefs represent their deeply felt reverence for the wonders of nature. Even rocks have spirits. (2) People throughout the ages have wished for supernatural powers, and for some people belief in such powers has become a wish-fulfillment. (3) If people cannot bring themselves to believe they have developed supernatural powers, they come to believe that their leaders have these powers. Then they can bask in the glory of their leaders and have their leaders perform the miracles they want. Shamans, priests, pharaohs, and kings have taken on this role. (4) The symbolic nature of our brain leads us to question why things happen and creates models to explain their causes. False models and supernatural fiction can result. (5) Myths, legends, rituals, and magic have been used to represent intense feelings and emotions that words alone cannot adequately represent. The snake is such an example. (6) Our desire for power and control to help us deal with adversity and quiet our survival anxiety can lead to the creation of supernatural beliefs. (7) supernatural beliefs are used to construct sacred self and group identities that enhance one's self and one's group, such as the myth of the master race in Nazi Germany (8) Our spiritual nature is encoded in our brains and can lift us beyond the material world. This can readily lead to the notion of spirits, angels, and a universal higher power.

Supernatural Beliefs and Survival Advantage

While the reasons given for the creation and use of supernatural beliefs seem credible, it is difficult to account for the perpetuation of these beliefs over thousands of years and their continued use in modern society in the face of scientific evidence to the contrary. What can account for the figures cited in Professor Pinker's book, that 69 percent of Americans believe in angels, 87 percent believe that Jesus was raised from the dead, and 96 percent believe in a God or universal spirit? Likewise, some recent polls have shown that an overwhelming majority of Americans believe in heaven, hell, and life after death. While many nonbelievers exist, they seem to be greatly outnumbered by believers.

One question that might be asked is whether belief in the supernatural or in supernatural powers confers any survival advantage over nonbelief. The question of survival advantage naturally leads to questions of health and recovery from illness, accidents, and other threats to life. A quote from Dr. Andrew Weil, who was previously cited, seems relevant to this discussion. He writes in his book, *Spontaneous Healing*:

> As an evolutionary necessity, organisms must have mechanisms of self-repair when injury or illness strikes. For most of our existence as a species, we have not had doctors, whether conventional, alternative or otherwise. The survival of the species alone implies the existence of a healing system.[8]

Since evolution and natural selection work over time, a long period of time is needed to evaluate how belief and nonbelief in supernatural powers might have affected the healing system and hence survival rates. Looking at the kind of medical practices that existed over a four-to-five-thousand-year period and how these practices interacted with supernatural or mystical beliefs is a good way to start. While some evidence of medical practices can be found in prehistoric artifacts, written evidence begins about five thousand years ago.

A Historical Look at Medicine and Supernatural Beliefs

It wasn't until the eighteenth and nineteenth centuries, however, that medicine finally began to stand on firm scientific ground. The circulation of blood was finally understood, microbes were revealed by the microscope, and the smallpox vaccine was introduced. *A History of Medicine* by Sutcliffe and Duin brings these points home, but it also goes back to the oldest medical record, dated 2150 BC, to show how the practice of medicine incorporated mystical and supernatural ideas before it became ruled by science.[9]

In ancient Mesopotamia, almost five thousand years ago, the medical profession consisted of both sorcerers and physicians; the former used charms and incantations, while the latter were involved in primitive first-aid and surgery. Babylonian medicine, thousands of years ago, combined ritual incantations, herbal remedies, and physical therapy; physicians identified the illness demons and drove them from the afflicted body. The ancient Hebrews, known for practicing cleanliness, nevertheless believed that diseases resulted from displeasing God and that only priests could help. Egyptian medicine was based on the belief that disease came from evil spirits that entered the body through the mouth, nose, and ears; sorcerers, exorcists, and magicians used incantations, amulets, spells, and ritual remedies.

Early Chinese medicine dealt almost exclusively with acupuncture, using fine needles on 365 points on the body; this was believed to treat diseases by allowing energy (chi) to enter and leave the body. Heart disease was treated with a concoction of octopus ink mixed with vinegar. In ancient India physicians believed that disturbances in breath, bile, phlegm, and blood were responsible for disease. Doctors used incantations but also performed primitive surgery like cauterizing fistulas, removing bladder and kidney stones, and sewing up wounds.

In ancient Greece the greatest of all doctors was Hippocrates, who emphasized the role of the environment in health. But like all Greek physicians, he based his medical practice on trying to balance the four humors of the body: blood, phlegm, yellow bile, and black bile, since imbalance was believed to cause disease. Patients also went to the asklepieia (temples), where they read about miraculous cures performed by the god Asklepios, the patron god of physicians.

Medical practice in Ancient Rome relied almost entirely on the Greek practice. During a plague in 293 BC., the Romans called upon Asklepias (Roman: Asculapius) for help. Galen, a Greek physician, arrived in Rome in AD 162 and advanced the Greek theory of the four humors to the point that it became both medical and Church dogma. He used bloodletting in order to balance the humors. The emperor Marcus Aurelius was one of his patients.

In the Middle Ages the Church became dominant and medicine became a matter of faith, with prayer being the most frequent prescription. The Church decreed that sickness was a consequence of sin, but took care of the sick as an act of Christian charity.

In the late 1320s a plague erupted in the Gobi desert of Mongolia, and within a generation it had spread to China, Russia, England, and Italy. The Church proclaimed that the plague, known as the Black Death, was God's punishment for the sinfulness of mankind. The plague wiped out about 25 percent of the European population. It took several more centuries to divorce medicine from religion and to support it with sound scientific principles. As late as the nineteenth century, superstition still had its place, as astrology played a part in deciding when to operate and when medication would be most effective. Thankfully, this practice was finally abandoned.

A Historical Look at Supernatural Faith-Based Practices

In addition to the practice of medicine, which concentrated on healing the body, historical records show that humans relied on supernatural entities and rituals to ensure good harvests, bring about healthy births, uplift people's spirits, save their souls, and guide them in the afterlife. Marcus Bach, professor of religion at the University of Iowa, in his book *Strange Sects and Curious Cults*, looks at the supernatural beliefs and practices that made up the ancient world—some of which are still in existence today. The ancient world was full of gods, goddesses, and sacred symbols that carried enormous power in the minds of believers.[10]

The worship of the god Baal, or Baalism, was prevalent about three thousand years before the time of Christ and was practiced throughout the Middle East. Many sexual rituals were involved. In ancient

Egypt, priests and pharaohs embodied the powers of Osiris, god of agriculture and of life and death. Golden staves and the ankh (a cross with a loop on top) were believed to carry magical power. The Greek culture was replete with gods and goddesses, and Mount Olympus was considered to be their home. With twelve Olympian deities, the Greeks had many opportunities to engage in supernatural practices. In the Roman Empire the god Bacchus oversaw many wild festivals, while the goddess Isis was honored as the patroness of motherhood and gave strength to women in childbirth and watched over their offspring. The Israelites were able to endure oppression at the hands of the Egyptians because of their faith in their one God and the belief that he would help them triumph over the forces of evil. The Old Testament contains the many miracles that they believed God performed for them.

The Christian faith, which also proclaims that only one God exists, follows the teachings of Christ—considered to be the Son of God—and spiritually baths in the many miracles he performed. The belief in Christ's resurrection and return as a savior is the foundation of Christianity. In India many sacred symbols venerate Shiva, one of the three gods in the Hindu trinity (which also includes Brahma, the creator, and Vishnu, the preserver). Early Hindus, like the early people of any land, personified and worshipped the passions they felt within themselves and the powers they saw in nature.

Throughout Africa, before the slave trade began, the people worshipped invisible spirits who were considered guardian angles and protectors and were referred to as the Loa. These spirits represented one great god, the Gran Mait, in a religion the French called vaudou. The Anglicized name became Voodoo after the slaves were exposed to Christianity in Haiti. Voodoo developed into a mixture of Christian, spiritualist, and animistic belief. The Haitian government officially outlawed Voodoo as a religion, but Voodoo services are still practiced.

While the above is not a complete historical account of all the ancient faith-based practices and does not cover the supernatural and magical rituals not involved with religion, it does cover the greater part of humanity and is sufficient for a further discussion of my thesis that supernatural beliefs are a manifestation of our symbolic brain.

Has Supernatural Belief Helped Us Survive?

When one looks at the medical and the faith-based practices outlined above, it is difficult to say which of these practices may have contributed to or detracted from the rate of human survival. Yet we certainly know that humans survived, regardless of what practices were embraced. Even the Black Death, which wiped out 25 percent of the European population, didn't wipe out 100 percent of the population. What contributed to the survival of the other 75 percent?

Nor was disease the only hazard that ancient cultures faced in the four thousand or so years before modern civilization took hold. Yet somehow humans survived, thrived, and have now populated the earth with close to seven billion individuals. How did humans manage it? In looking at the various beliefs and practices embracing the supernatural, it would be interesting to consider their impact on natural selection. This will be attempted in the coming chapters by utilizing the studies and findings outlined in the previous chapters, which focused on the positive and negative placebo effects, the effect of stress, and the symbolic expression of emotion and action.

CHAPTER V

Supernatural Beliefs and Natural Selection

It Didn't Help! What Do I Do Now?

Have humans changed very much since the beginning of recorded history some six thousand years ago? The tenets of *The Psychological Immune System* proclaim that the innate nature of humans has remained the same, but that we have acquired much more knowledge and changed our beliefs over and over again as groups, societies, cultures, and nationalities have changed. Our unchanged innate nature is to protect, preserve, and enhance the lives, physical well-being, property and possessions, and the sense of self and identity of ourselves and those we love.[1] But the methods we have learned and the technologies we have developed to do so have been transformed quite a bit.

When disease strikes and threatens our lives or those of our loved ones, when we lose our property or possessions, or when humiliation and loss of status come upon us or our loved ones, strong emotional reactions arise and we desperately search for ways to handle them—now and six thousand years ago! We tap into our own learned resources, and if that doesn't work reach out to others and to socially sanctioned avenues of dealing with the threats and losses. We do whatever we can and hope that an answer to our problems comes from somewhere—now and six thousand years ago. The human response to what doesn't work remains the same. "It didn't help! What do I do now?"

What Did People Do in Ancient Egypt?

Seth woke up one day and said to his wife, Mery, "I'm not feeling too good. I have this tightness in my chest like someone is pushing down on me." Mery responded, "Does it hurt? Are you in lots of pain?" "No," said Seth, "but it doesn't feel too good, and I don't think I can make it to the quarry today. I'm going to have to let the governor know that I'm not coming in today. Could you walk over to Honus's house and tell him to let the governor know about me when he goes to work?" "All right, Seth," said Mery. "I'll be back in about fifteen minutes."

While his wife was away Seth considered what could have brought about the tightness in his chest and his lack of energy. He figured that the heavy work at the quarry could be at fault. "After all," he thought, "I'm going on thirty-three years of age, and maybe I should be thinking about retiring." He knew the average life span was about thirty-five or so, and that he was feeling his age after fifteen years at the quarry.

When Mery returned, Seth asked her to rub his chest with a commonly used concoction of mashed cloves of garlic in olive oil. She proceeded to do that, and after about thirty minutes he felt better. Unfortunately, the next day the same feeling of pressure on his chest returned and he also had shortness of breath and felt a little nauseous.

He decided he had better consult the physician at the quarry and ask for his diagnosis.

He went over to Honus's house and that morning they caught a boat to the quarry. Seth told the physician what he was experiencing and what he had done so far. The physician pushed on different parts of Seth's chest to find out which area was most sensitive. He took Seth's pulse and listened to his labored breathing. He told Seth that when the River Nile becomes blocked, crops become unhealthy, and that people, like the river, had channels that carry air, water, and blood to different parts of the body and that at times these channels become blocked through either spoiled food or malicious demons. He told Seth to try unblocking these channels by taking a laxative and see if that helped. If that didn't clear up the pressure, nausea, and shortness of breath, then he would have to assume that some demons were causing the block-age. This would require the right religious rituals and incantations to drive the demons from the body.

He told Seth to take few days off and promised to let the governor of the province know about Seth's problem. He was sure the governor would approve of his plan for Seth, and said that if the problem had not cleared up in a few days then Seth should come back to see him again. So Seth returned home and told his wife what the physician had said and done. She seemed relieved that he had gone to get help, and said to him, "I'm less anxious now than I was before." Seth too felt better for the visit and knew that if he still felt bad the physician was ready and able to take care of his problem by getting rid of his demons.

While Seth and his wife had confidence in the physician at the quarry and were pleased with his recommendations, it is possible that when a prescribed treatment didn't work, an Egyptian could lose his confidence in the treating physician-priest and end up a skeptic. This parallels modern society, and the same question was asked six thousand years ago as is still asked today when things don't work: "What do I do now?"

What Was Seth's Problem?

The symptoms listed for Seth were taken from the chapter on the heart by Drs. Barry Massie and Thomas Amidon in *Current Medical Diagnosis & Treatment*.[2] They say, "The commonest cause of cardiac chest pain is myocardial ischemia (a reduction of oxygen to the heart). This is usually described as dull, aching, or as a sensation of 'pressure,' 'tightness,' 'squeezing,' or 'gas,' rather than as sharp or spasmodic; and it is often perceived as an uncomfortable sensation rather than 'pain.' Ischemic pain usually subsides within 30 minutes but may last longer." Nausea and shortness of breath are also listed as possible symptoms.

The medical practices of ancient Egypt, some of which were described in the previous chapter, were taken from a number of additional sources.[3,4,5] Since the ancient Egyptians didn't know the symptoms of heart disease or how the heart worked, they did the best they could based on faulty medical knowledge. The population had to either believe what they were told by the physician-priests or be skeptical of what they were told, either of which could have contributed to the treatment's outcome. More than likely there was a range of reactions, with some people willing to bet their life on the treatment and others maintaining much doubt.

What Did People Do in Ancient Greece?

Alexis had just finished trying out for the Olympic Games and was pretty tired when he got home. His wife, Sophia, was glad he was home and gave him a big hug. She drew him a warm bath, helped scrub him down, and prepared the bed for him just as she was expected to do as his wife. He thanked her and went to bed. When Alexis awoke the next morning, he felt a tickle in his throat and was coughing a little. Sophia made him the usual breakfast of barley bread dipped in wine and gave him olives on the side. She suggested that he take a glass of the special medicinal wine they had stored, which might help his cough. He agreed and drank a glass of the special wine, which had thyme and other herbs mixed into it. After breakfast he said that he was going to see his friend Jason, and that they might go sailing. He bid Sophia farewell, and off he went.

Alexis returned home in time for dinner, but his coughing had increased and he felt very warm. Sophia touched her hand to his head and said she thought he had a fever. Alexis replied that fever was known to cook the bad humors, helping the body get rid of them and restoring the proper balance of the humors. So he would let the fever be. He figured he would be better by tomorrow if his humors were restored to balance. Sophia said she had dinner waiting for him, consisting of bean soup and grilled tuna. Alexis said he really wasn't that hungry because of all the coughing and congestion, but that he would try a little of each. He topped off his dinner with some more medicinal wine and decided to go to bed, hoping to get some sleep and wake up feeling better.

The next morning Alexis was still coughing, unhappily, and found that he was coughing up some blood. He told Sophia that he should see his physician. She asked if she could go along, and he told her that she could. So they both walked the quarter-mile to where the physician had his office. They walked in, sat in the waiting room, and waited their turn. The physician finally took Alexis in but had Sophia stay in the waiting room. He listened to Alexis's description of his problem, put his ear to Alexis's chest, felt his forehead, had him cough into a small urn, and took his pulse. He examined the sputum and blood in the urn and told Alexis that he had an inflammation of the lungs, or peripneumonia (which we now call "pneumonia").

He explained to Alexis that he had accumulated an excess of phlegm and blood in his lungs, and that this had caused the humors in his body to fall out of balance. He went on to assert that in order to balance the black bile and yellow bile with the phlegm and blood, Alexis needed to get rid of the extra phlegm and blood in his lungs. He told Alexis that this would take some time, as it would require an expectorant medication to reduce the phlegm, the withdrawal of blood or bloodletting to get rid of the stagnant blood, and daily visits to the asklepieia or temple where the god Asklepios resided. He asked Alexis how he felt about his guidance? Alexis said that his illness sounded serious and that he was willing to do whatever might help cure him. The physician said that peripneumonia was indeed a serious condition, but that by following his treatment plan Alexis could restore the balance of humors in his body and regain his health. He told Alexis to come back the next day for the first bloodletting session.

Alexis thanked the physician and left, went to the waiting room and picked up Sophia, and walked back home while explaining to her what the physician had said about his condition and the treatment. She asked him if he had confidence in the physician, and Alexis said he did. Would it have made any difference in the healing process if Alexis had told Sophia that he had some but not total confidence in the physician? What if he had told Sophia that he would follow the treatment plan, but had little confidence in the physician?

What Was Alexis's Problem?

The symptoms listed for Alexis were taken from a section on the lung by John L. Stauffer, M.D., professor of medicine at the Pennsylvania State University College of Medicine, which was included in the book *Current Medical Diagnosis and Treatment*.[6] Dr. Stauffer states that the symptoms of pneumonia include chills, high fever, chest pain, and a purulent (pus-filled) cough that often produces bloody sputum. He goes on to say that mortality is high unless treated with antibiotics. The medical practices of ancient Greece were gleaned from a number of sources[8,9,10] in addition to the material taken from *A History of Medicine* mentioned in the previous chapter.

While the physicians of ancient Greece were aware of lung inflammation or pneumonia, they had no idea that it was caused by bacteria and so had no way of eliminating the causative agent. Any cure would have had to depend on the ability of the immune system to eventually destroy the bacteria. More than likely some people with pneumonia survived despite the misguided ideas of treatment, and it's likely that those who had the most faith in the physicians and the god Asklepios had the best chance of surviving.

What Did People Do in Ancient China?

If Khan, a resident of ancient China, had the same symptoms as Seth of ancient Egypt, would a Chinese physician have known what caused these symptoms? What kind of examination and treatment could Khan expect from a practicing physician?

Since the conceptual framework of ancient Chinese medicine was based on maintaining balance in the body of yin (the dark, moist, female force) and yang (the bright, dry, male force), the physician examining Khan would have tried to determine what had caused an imbalance of his yin and yang to produce his symptoms. He would have paid extraordinary attention to the pulse in both of Kahn's arms to determine whether his blood flowed freely and evenly, and he would have considered what organs were influencing Khan's pulse and what changes in his body might be causing the symptoms. This examination could have taken hours to complete. It is possible that the physician would have implicated Khan's heart as producing the symptoms and imbalances, but he would probably have pointed to the lungs and stomach as well.

As for treatment, the physician would have prescribed medication, acupuncture, moxibustion (the burning of a powdered substance on Khan's skin, causing a blister), and massage. Heart medication could have been octopus ink mixed with vinegar, ephedra might have been prescribed for Khan's shortness of breath, and ginseng for his nausea.[11,12] If Khan's symptoms were reduced or eliminated by this treatment, he might have become a disciple of Chinese medicine.

What Did People Do in Ancient India?

If Mori, an inhabitant of ancient India, had shown the same symptoms of pneumonia as Alexis of Greece, would Indian physicians have recognized these symptoms? And what type of examination and treatment could Mori expect?

Indian physicians were trained in Ayurvedic medicine, which was based on the beliefs and teachings of the Aryans, who moved into India around 1500 BC and left a body of literature known as the Vedas (Sanskrit for knowledge). The Atharva-Veda contains references to disease and health but also stresses spells and incantations for the practice of magic. Omens played a large part in the diagnosis of an illness, as did observation of a patient's sputum, urine, stool, and vomitus.[13]

Mori would have been examined and it would have been noted that he had a fever and was coughing up sputum and blood. The physician would have assumed that the levels of the four primary substances— wind, bile, phlegm, and blood—that make up a healthy individual were not in balance, or that the three doshas (biological humors or psychophysiological energies) called vata, pitta, and kapha were not in balance. The physician would have tried to restore the balance by eliminating the symptoms. Mori would have been given ginger and honey to eliminate his cough and treat his fever, and an incantation would have been made to reduce the blood and sputum being coughed up.[14,15]

Since the doctors would have had no knowledge that bacteria were causing pneumonia, a cure would have had to depend on the strength of Mori's immune system, which would have been influenced by his trust in the doctor and his belief in the effectiveness of the treatment. If the treatment had failed to work, Mori might have been added to the ranks of the doubters and disbelievers, if not of the deceased.

How Natural Selection Fits In

The evidence and stories cited in Chapter III clearly indicate that one's beliefs—no matter whether true or false— evokes emotional responses that trigger biochemical reactions that can affect one's immune, nervous, and endocrine systems. This interactional chain underlies the placebo, nacebo, and anxiety responses leading, at times, to unpredictable and astounding recoveries or setbacks. As Deric Bownds remarks in his book *The Biology of Mind*, "The mind-body connection reaches down to the intricate details of our immune system biochemistry."[16]

The treatment of Seth for heart problems in ancient Egypt and the treatment of Khan for his heart problems in ancient China, although unscientific medical procedures, could possibly have produced good outcomes. Similarly, the treatment of Alexis for pneumonia in ancient Greece and the treatment of Mori for pneumonia in ancient India, while sounding pretty farfetched, could also have produced good results.

A common belief among all the above medical procedures and rituals is that some imbalance in the body must be corrected to cure diseases. This thinking parallels the modern conviction in medical science that a homeostatic system maintains a healthy balance among the systems of the body, just as a thermostat controls the temperature balance in a building. If this belief in balance was internalized by the patients in the ancient cultures, then it may have functioned as a placebo effect or provided relief from anxiety.

In addition to the medical procedures and beliefs that people were exposed to in ancient civilizations, they were also exposed to the supernatural beliefs and practices that were part of the countries in which they lived. Ancient Egypt had Osiris, god of life and death. Ancient Greece had its gods and goddesses on Mount Olympus, while India had the Hindu trinity of Shiva, Brahma, and Vishnu. There were also magical symbols and rituals that one could follow for protection and self-preservation. Many of these magical symbols and rituals have survived through the ages and can still be found in the twenty-first century. Those used by the Eveny people of Siberia and the followers of Voodoo in Haiti are examples.

Many studies and observations point to the fact that not everyone benefits to the same degree from the placebo effect, just as not everyone feels the same degree of trauma in response to a stressful event or recovers as quickly as everyone else. It is estimated that about 15 percent of a population are high responders (benefiting the most), 15 percent are low responders (benefiting the least), and the rest fall in between. This means that no matter what treatments were used in the ancient world for heart problems or pneumonia—or any other disease— those who had the most faith in the physician and in the healing effect of their treatment benefited the most. The same could be said for those who suffered from stress: those who had the most faith in practitioners of religion or in the religion itself could reduce their stress the most. Those who claimed to possess supernatural powers and could convince others of their powers probably were able to help both the sick and the stressed-out.

The Carrying on of Beliefs

Knowing that both sickness and stress can lead to untimely death, it follows that those individuals who believed most strongly in the practitioners lived the longest. In the ancient world, living to the age of thirty-five was an accomplishment. Adding to one's age meant that a family could produce more offspring. So natural selection was on the side of the strongest believers, and they had the longest opportunity to instill their beliefs in the minds of their children. Once our symbolic brain formulates a model of the world and how it operates, the belief persists tenaciously. So the belief goes from parent to child, and from the child to future children in turn.

Suppose we divided up the ancient population six thousand years ago into the believers and the doubters of the medical treatments and supernatural interventions. What would their ratio look like after four thousand years if it started out as a fifty-fifty split between believers (B) and doubters (D)?

Since natural selection would be on the side of B, more of them would survive to procreate than D. If one percent more B survived than D over a two hundred-year-period, the ratio would be 51 percent B and 49 percent D. After four hundred years we would have 52 percent B and 48 percent D. Over one thousand years B would be in the middle 50 percent and D in the middle 40s. After two thousand years the population would be near 60 percent B and 40 percent D. After four thousand years we would be looking at a population of B in the low 70 percent and D in the low 30s. By the nineteenth century, B would make up about 75 percent and D about 25 percent. Eventually, when medicine became more scientific, diagnosis more exact, and medication more specific to the causative agents of disease, then strong belief in non-scientific treatment, miracles, and the supernatural would not be as important a factor in determining the outcome of a treatment. Thus, believers would have little or no advantage over doubters or nonbelievers. For example, if a patient had pneumonia, then treatment with antibiotics would be more beneficial than treatment with bloodletting or ginger and honey, no matter how strongly the patient believed in the latter treatment.

Hanging on to Beliefs

The fact that modern medicine rests on more testable, scientific knowledge about the human body doesn't mean that people of the nineteenth, twentieth, and twenty-first centuries were willing to give up their belief in miracles, the supernatural, religious practitioners, and alternative treatments. As stated above, when beliefs about preserving and enhancing one's life and sense of self are passed down from parents to children, they become difficult to ease; they are core beliefs. So once natural selection took its toll on doubters and established believers as the overwhelming majority, the majority became permanent and it looks like it will remain so.

There are still diseases like cancer and AIDS that medicine hasn't cured; there are still traumatic events in people's lives that are difficult to erase; there is still the bewilderment about and difficulty accepting the phenomena of death and dying; and there still exists the natural tendency to think about and conceptualize the spiritual side of life. Relaxation techniques, self-help groups, plus antianxiety and antidepressive medications have now been passed on to the public to help people cope. But doubters still have difficulty competing with those who believe in the hereafter, miracles, spirits, angels, religious rituals, and prayer. It seems that when people get stressed out, worry about their future, and search for salvation, they still tend to rely on belief to help maintain their sense of stability, self-confidence, and hopes for a better future.

How Our Symbolic Brain Fits In

Given the misguided medical treatments in the ancient world, and considering that supernatural beliefs were part of these treatments, it may seem hard to believe that people survived and thrived. This can be attributed to our symbolic brain, which can achieve real physical results using imagination, conceptual models, and abstractions that have little or no connections to reality. As long as we believe what we imagine or are told is real, then it becomes real to us. How is it that evolution has given us a brain that can accept false ideas and fantasies as reality and use them to govern our actions? Wouldn't such a brain lead us to make grievous mistakes and place our very survival at risk? This is what the next chapter will look at.

CHAPTER VI

Supernatural Beliefs and Human Survival

The Power of Belief

Based on the studies cited in previous chapters, it is clear that beliefs trigger emotions that can vitally affect the immune, endocrine, and nervous systems. These, in turn, are tied up intimately with life, physical well-being, and survival. Evolution and natural selection, it seems, have determined that connecting belief to emotion and emotion to regulatory systems is biologically sound. The placebo and nacebo effects are examples of what our beliefs can bring about. In addition, how much stress we experience and how long stress persists also depends to a large extent on what we believe about the situations that cause the stress and how much we believe in our own ability to handle them.

When we are confronted by challenges, obstacles, or threats to our life, property, or sense of self, our emotions arouse our symbolic brain, which tries to comprehend the circumstances that confront us. It looks at what we are up against, it produces verbal and visual models—which may or may not be accurate—and creates plans of how to deal with the challenges, obstacles, and threats.

In the last chapter I tried to show that, in the ancient world, if people had faith in medical practitioners and their treatments, even mistaken beliefs could produce both positive and negative results. Faith in positive outcomes elicited the placebo effect, and belief in negative outcomes—which evoked fear—produced the nacebo effect. In addition, faith in the religious practices and supernatural rituals of the ancient world had a stress-reducing effect. In this way, as long as people believed in the practices or rituals used, the models created by their symbolic brains didn't have to be accurate in order to be helped by them. Their beliefs put them more at ease with the problems they faced and assured them that they could overcome the problems, or that they could call on powerful figures to help them.

Making Sense and Nonsense

What dipping into the ancient world of medicine, religion, and supernatural practices showed us is that our symbolic brain tries to make sense of things when faced with challenges and problems. And its workings today are no different. The ideas or models that emerge may be different, but the attempt to understand things is the same. That's the nature of our symbolic brain.

This model of our symbolic brain fits in nicely with my concept of a psychological immune system, which, I believe, has evolved to protect, preserve, and enhance the human species. In fact, I see the symbolic brain as an adjunct to and a component of the psychological immune system, for it too is driven by emotions to create ideas, models, and symbolic systems to help protect, preserve, and enhance life, property, and sense of self. It doesn't even require a conscious intent in order to get it to work; sometimes solutions come to mind when one is not even focused on the problem.

Making sense of things is a very important function of our symbolic brain, and a scientific understanding of the world has been one result. But our minds also create fantasies and science fiction to explain things that science cannot. There is no limit to our imagination, which can produce supernatural musings as well as creative theories, models, and inventions.

Making Sense of Disease

The germ theory of disease developed by Louis Pasteur in 1862 replaced all the past models of what caused disease.[1] It replaced the belief that disease was a punishment from God for bad behavior; that malicious demons were blocking channels carrying air, water, and blood to the body; that the humors of black bile, yellow bile, phlegm, and blood were out of balance; and that the doshas of vita, pitta, and kapha were not in balance. At the time these models of disease made sense to medical practitioners and their patients, but now they are considered nonsense. If a physician used these models today, he would be accused of malpractice.

Yet despite the fact that modern medicine is backed by pretty solid science, some people still believe that disease can be cured by prayer, supernatural rituals, or magical incantations. The placebo and nacebo effects can still be elicited by these ancient practices but the consequences of relying solely on the supernatural route can also be deadly. For example, an article in the *Denver*

Post related that a thirteen-year-old girl died of complications from untreated diabetes because her parents belonged to a church that believed in prayer rather than medical treatment, and that other children of this church have also died because medical treatment was withheld. Some members of this church have been prosecuted in the past for withholding medical treatment, but in order to prosecute, the district attorney has to prove that the parents knew the severity of their children's condition. This can be difficult to prove.[2]

Then there is a type of faith-healing and energy medicine known as consegrity, which seems to repeat what was believed in the past. Consegrity holds that energy fields surround the body's organs and that these energy fields must be kept in balance to maintain health; when the balance is disrupted, the body breaks down. The practice of consegrity admonishes people to avoid others who give out negative energy and be with people who have positive energy. One of the founders of this system was Debra Harrison, a massage therapist who died in the summer of 2005 while being treated with consegrity for diabetes. Believers in consegrity blamed Harrison's death on her nephew and other family members because of the negative energy they emitted while trying to persuade her to go to the hospital for treatment.[3]

There was also a study reported in the medical journal *Pediatrics*, which said that of 172 children's deaths in families who practiced faith-healing, 140 were the result of conditions whose survival rates exceed 90 percent with medical care.[4] Here again, reliance on faith-healing had dire consequences when modern medical practices were available but refused.

The development of technology and experimentation have allowed further refinement of the theory of disease, and according to the psychological immune system, discovery will continue, for we are programmed to protect, preserve, and enhance our life and physical well-being.[5] Our symbolic brain is part of this program and will continue to churn out ideas, theories, and models to further clarify the nature of disease. We must remember, however, that what makes sense today may be deemed nonsense in the future.

Making Sense of Our Gods

Not too long ago we humans believed in and prayed to a multitude of gods, both male and female, who ruled over different aspects of the world. Each had his or her own powers; they competed with each other, fought with each other, and even cohabitated with each other. Nowadays in the West, all of these gods have been replaced by the belief in one God. Polytheism has been pushed aside as nonsense and replaced by monotheism, which is considered the true nature of things.

Our prayers now go out to one God (the same God?) in Judaism, Christianity, and Islam. Hinduism seems to have one main god and a number of minor gods, who could be considered comparable to the saints and angels of Christianity.[6] Although atheism (there is no God) is also a belief that has often been voiced in the current century, it is not shared by the overwhelming majority of the nearly seven billion humans who now inhabit our planet.

All religions, even anti-religious atheism, seem to stem from the human desire to understand our place in the universe. The gifts of consciousness and self-awareness, which evolution has bestowed on us, have placed a burden on our symbolic brain to come up with answers to questions about why we are here and where we are headed. Is there a bright future ahead, or is Armageddon right around the corner? Why do we keep looking for answers? Because that's the nature of our symbolic brain.

Making Sense of the Starry Sky

If you've had the experience of seeing the night sky without any city lights, perhaps while camping, boating, or hiking, you're surely aware that this awe-inspiring sight can be a source of fascination and wonder. Early man could look up and see the star-filled sky on a nightly basis and must have been intrigued by the different patterns of stars and frightened by the "falling stars" (meteorites) that appeared on a regular basis. His senses and emotions would have been strongly aroused and would have kindled his symbolic brain to come up with a formulation of what was going on. It is not hard to imagine that supernatural forces would have been considered to explain such grand, wondrous, and overwhelming sights.

Dividing the sky up into constellations—which is still employed by modern astronomy—and making them relevant to human life would be in keeping with early man's attempt to protect, preserve, and enhance his own existence. Take the constellations of the Big Dipper (Ursa Major) and Orion, which are prominent patterns in the maze of stars. Were these constellations seen as mere random patterns of stars? No, they were seen as supernatural figures placed in the sky by the gods.

The Big Dipper, for example, was imagined to be a bear. One story goes that the bear represented Callisto, a daughter of the King of Arcadia, who was loved by the god Jupiter. In order to protect her, he turned her into a bear and put her into the sky. A second story is that the Great Spirit put the Great Bear in the sky to act as a "calendar" for earthly bears. During the winter months, when the Great Bear is low in the sky, earthly bears stay in their dens and keep warm. When the Great Bear moves high in the sky, summer begins and the earthly bears leave their dens.

The constellation Orion was seen as a hunter holding a club in one hand and a lion skin in the other, and wearing a belt with a sword attached. A story goes that Orion boasted that no animal could overcome him. To challenge him Jupiter sent a scorpion, which ended up killing him. The goddess Diana pitied Orion and transferred him to the sky as far away from the Scorpion (another constellation) as possible, or halfway across the sky.[7]

The constellations also figured strongly in astrology. Thousands of years ago early man gave special preference to a band-shaped section of the sky known as the zodiac, whose twelve constellations were given astrological signs. The belief was—and for many people still is—that persons are strongly influenced by whichever of the twelve signs they are born under, and that their personalities and behavior stem from the power of the associated constellation. For example, anyone born from March 21 to April 19 has Aries as his sign and the ram as his symbol. An Aries is supposed to be bold, energetic, and strong-willed, and ruled by the planet Mars. People born between July 23 and August 22 have Leo as their sign and the lion as their symbol. They are believed to be energetic and strong-willed with kingly qualities, and they enjoy being the center of attention. They are ruled by the sun. Individuals born between September 23 and October 22 have Libra as their sign and a pair of weighing scales as their symbol. Libras like balance and harmony in all things and dislike conflict, disagreement, and sudden changes. They often have trouble making up their minds because they are quick to listen to and understand different viewpoints. They are ruled by the planet Venus. Anyone can fit in.

Individual horoscopes eventually became popular and astrologers became predictors of people's futures. Astrologers still exist today. People still go to them for astrological readings and consult their horoscopes before taking important actions or making plans for the future.[8] As a matter of fact, it is well known that former First Lady Nancy Reagan consulted an astrologer to determine what were the best times for President Ronald Reagan to travel or carry out serious activities. White House Chief of Staff Donald Reagan, in his book *For the Record*, wrote, "Virtually every major move and decision the Reagans made during my time as White House Chief of Staff was cleared in advance with a woman in San Francisco who drew up horoscopes to make certain that the planets were in a favorable alignment for the enterprise."[9]

Early man's brain and modern man's brain work the same way. Both have the job of understanding and explaining how the things they see and experience came to be. Before the science of astronomy became established, how were humans able to explain what stars were, how they came to be, and what relationship they had to humans? They turned to the supernatural and to the gods who they believed controlled their lives and that of the stars. What else could explain such a vast and wondrous sight? The same type of imagination is still found today in science fiction stories and in supernatural beliefs like reincarnation, ghosts, angels, and possession by the devil.

Based on the science of astronomy, we now know that stars are made up of mainly hydrogen and helium and some heavy metals, which burn at extremely high temperatures. Astronomer Cecelia Payne is credited with discovering the composition of stars by studying their spectra and was awarded the prestigious Henry Norris Russell Prize in 1976. In her acceptance lecture she maintained that the reward of the young scientist is the thrill of being the first person in history to see something or to understand something.[10]

Her symbolic brain was doing what all of our brains continually do: forming concepts, models, and formulations that make the most sense of what we see and experience. This is the underlying basis of our survival, even though many mistaken ideas have arisen along the way. Astronomy has introduced the "big bang" theory to explain how our universe got started. It hasn't, however, explained where the initial energy or mass came from that exploded into the universe, so the idea of God or some supernatural force as the prime mover can still be entertained by our minds until further knowledge is accumulated that negates a supernatural force.

Making Sense of Global Warming

Our beliefs can determine our destiny and that of our children, grandchildren, their children, and future generations. Our belief about global warming carries such a consequence. If it is truly happening, as a substantial number of scientists believe, and nothing is done to stop it, then our very survival is at stake. If it is not happening, as a smaller number of people believe, then believers are being unnecessarily frightened and hoodwinked into dealing with a non-existent threat. This can produce prolonged anxiety and a waste of our resources.

Rush Limbaugh, a radio talk-show host who claims to have at least thirty million listeners, talks about global warming as a hoax perpetrated on the general public by liberal pseudo-scientists, politicians, and their followers. He believes that liberals are playing people like suckers. When asked why anyone would want to perpetrate such a hoax on the public, his answer is that liberals want the government to have absolute power so conservatism can be destroyed and they alone can rule the nation. By scaring the public they can get people to rely on the government for their well-being, and thus create total dependency. He claims it's a quest for power, pure and simple.

The propaganda about global warming and climate change is science fiction, Limbaugh believes, and belongs with other made-up fairy tales. He maintains that the false belief about global warming is created intentionally to stoke the public's fear and that once the public realizes this, they will run the deceivers like Al Gore out of town.

There are even some scientists who are skeptical about global warming or who doubt that, if it does exist, mankind is responsible for it, although they don't necessarily subscribe to the liberal conspiracy theory of Rush Limbaugh. For example, Dr. Timothy Ball, a former climatology professor at the University of Winnipeg, states, "I was also opposed to the threats of impending doom global cooling engendered as I am to the threats made about global warming. Let me stress I am not denying the phenomenon has occurred. The world has warmed since 1680, the nadir of a cool period called the Little Ice Age (LIA), that has generally continued to the present. These climate changes are well within the natural variability and explained quite easily by changes in the sun. But there is nothing unusual going on."[11]

Then there is David Bellamy, a botanist, naturalist, and author, who doesn't believe in man-made global warming and who states that he has been shunned by bosses at the BBC because of his views. He writes, "When I first stuck my head above the parapet to say I didn't believe what we were being told about global warming I had no idea what the consequences would be. I am a scientist and I have to follow the dictates of science, but when I see that the truth is being covered up I have to voice my opinion." He maintains that world temperatures have been getting colder since 1998 and that Arctic ice actually increased in 2002.[12]

In opposition to Rush Limbaugh and the scientists who doubt that global warming is occurring or that it is accelerated by human activity, an open letter was recently sent to the United States Congress from eighteen leading scientific organizations, including the American Association for the Advancement of Science, the American Geophysical Union, and the American Meteorological Society, giving their opinion about global warming. The letter states:[13]

Observations throughout the world make it clear that climate change is occurring, and rigorous scientific research demonstrates that the greenhouse gases emitted by human activities are the primary driver. These conclusions are based on multiple independent lines of evidence, and contrary assertions are inconsistent with an objective assessment of the vast body of peer-reviewed science. If we are to avoid the most severe impacts of climate change, emissions of greenhouse gases must be dramatically reduced.

So the question now becomes: are global warming and climate change fairy tales spread by liberals, or factual accounts of what is happening to the earth we live on? My vote is with the eighteen scientific societies, and my opinion is that the conspiracy theory of Rush Limbaugh is the real fairy tale, arising from an over-imaginative brain that finds it hard to distinguish between fact and fiction. This is a condition that has always plagued the human species, unfortunately, and one we all have to contend with because of the makeup of our symbolic brain.

Making Sense of Imagination and Fantasy

When it comes to imagination and fantasy, there are no greater creators than young children. In a recent book called *Supersense: Why We Believe in the Unbelievable*, neuroscientist Bruce M. Hood points out that children are natural-born fantasy creators[14]. He writes, "The children Piaget studied believed that trees have minds and can feel. In short, they thought the inanimate world is alive, something Piaget called 'animism.' Where do children get these ideas? No one tells them to think like this. It's just the way the child makes sense of the world."

Hood concludes that "The origins of supernatural beliefs are within every developing child" and that "adult supernaturalism is the residue of childhood misconceptions that have not been truly disposed of." He goes on to say that our mind is shaped in such a way that we search for the essence of things or the basic quality of an object or person and believe that this essence stays with the object or person. At a subliminal or unconscious level we feel that if we are in contact with an object or person, that essence can "rub off" on us. He maintains that this is why we want to be near and to touch famous people and celebrities, and why we are reluctant or even repulsed to wear the jacket of a murderer even after it has been dry cleaned. Would you wear the jacket of Jeffrey Dahmer—the man who killed and ate his victims? Would you sleep in the bed of a murder victim, even if the mattress and sheets had been changed? These are examples of how we are all primed to believe that magical and unnatural things can occur.

David Dow, interviewed by Terry Gross on "Fresh Air" for National Public Radio on February 9, 2010, described how the essence of one's surroundings can feel like it is being absorbed by or rubbed off onto you. Mr. Dow is an appellate court attorney in Texas who represents inmates on death row in order to get their sentences commuted to life in prison or to get them a new trial if he believes they are innocent. As part of this work he goes to the penitentiary to interview the prisoners and take notes. This can take many hours and can be a daily routine. He told Terry Gross that the first thing he does when he gets home is to throw his clothes in the washing machine and then take a shower. She asked him if he does this because the prison is unkempt and dirty, and he answered that the prison is actually rather clean and sanitary.

Why then, did he throw his clothes in the washing machine and take a shower? His answer was a little startling: "I just don't want the aura of death row to follow me into the house." He explained that he had a wife and kids to protect, and what he did gave him some assurance that he was ridding himself of the death row aura and keeping it out of the house. This superstitious feeling is the "supersense" that author Bruce Hood refers to, which resides in all children and continues to make its appearance in adults.

It is interesting to note that the Eveny people of Siberia, whom I discussed in Chapter IV, share beliefs that are similar to those of the children Piaget studied. They are convinced that rivers, lakes, forests, and rocks are alive, with their own souls and spirits giving them some degree of consciousness like our own. It seems to help them survive because they pay particular attention to their surroundings. The anthropologist Vitebsky, who wrote about them, emphasizes that they strive to be aware of the moods of their surroundings and adjust their behavior accordingly in order to achieve their aims and avoid disaster.[15]

Making Sense of Our Belief System

As we have seen, despite scientific and technical advances in medicine, many people still rely on faith and faith-healing as their preferred way of treating illness. It is also possible to rely on present-day medical practice but to resort to faith when medicine does not provide a cure. It seems that we can hold contradictory beliefs without considering ourselves abnormal or mentally disordered. Perhaps it could be better to say that we can hold dual beliefs and use the one that suits us best as circumstances dictate.

As previously stated, our symbolic brain can and does churn out varied models of the world, and someone has to choose which one is closer to the truth. If enough people accept a particular model, our tendency is to adopt that model. This is what occurred when the concept of supernatural and mystical forces took the form of many gods and finally one God. However, some people still accept multiple gods. But it is also possible not to believe in a God or gods, and still be accepted socially. Some members of society carry around doubts but pray when the going gets too tough. This may not sit well with strong believers, but it is possible to go through life being unsure. Still, some people are sure to push for a single belief with the question, "But what do you really believe?" or "Why can't you make up your mind?" As long as society allows divergent viewpoints, there will be divergent viewpoints, even in the same individual.

Science is strongly established in the twenty-first century, and most people accept its findings. Astronomy has really come into its own with the Hubble Space Telescope taking spectacular pictures of galaxies billions of light-years away. Our galaxy is one of billions, and our solar system is a tiny entity in our galaxy revolving around the sun, which is just one of the billions of stars in our galaxy. Despite this vast knowledge, some of us are still able to accept the ancient myth of astrology. Can both the facts of astronomy and the beliefs of astrology reside in the same brain? Yes, because one can be understood as the progress of science and the other can be seen as wisdom derived from the mystic interaction between humans and the heavens. One has to hope that rocket launching doesn't have to depend on astrology charts.

The controversy over global warming and the need to challenge the theory of evolution with creationism and intelligent design are also prime examples of how beliefs can influence and affect human society and survival. Fighting over beliefs is like fighting over property and possessions. In fact, beliefs can be thought of as our intellectual property, which natural selection has deemed worthy to protect and preserve according to the theory of the psychological immune system. What is truth to one person is a fairy tale to another. Others straddle the opposing beliefs and say they can't make up their minds or haven't yet been able to do so.

While an open society like ours allows many different beliefs to be held, it is up to those individuals in power to endorse some and reject others. We can accept children entertaining beliefs that border on the magical and supernatural, but how flexible is society in accepting adults who carry around and express the same magical and supernatural beliefs? This is an area certainly worth exploring, as we shall do in the next chapter.

CHAPTER VII

Professional and Societal Reactions to Supernatural Beliefs

When Do Beliefs Take on an Abnormal Flavor?

We can easily accept children's unbridled imagination and fantasies, because we realize that their minds are still being shaped and are wide open to fanciful ideas and speculations about the world around them. But how about adults who believe that rocks have a spirit and that fire can predict the future, as the Eveny believe? Do these beliefs border on a psychological disorder, or are they acceptable when they are shared by the whole community and don't seem to interfere with carrying out one's duties or maintaining an acceptable lifestyle?

When beliefs produce a social or occupational dysfunction then they could be viewed as bordering on a mental disorder. In fact, producing a dysfunction is one of the hallmarks of mental disorders as defined by the *Diagnostic and Statistical Manual of Mental Disorders, Fourth Edition (DSM-IV)*. For example, in order to classify a fearful belief as a phobia, a hopeless feeling as a depression, or a fantasy as psychotic in nature, they all must "interfere significantly with the person's normal routine, occupational functioning, or social activities or relationships."[1]

This implies that one can maintain beliefs of a magical or supernatural nature without being considered mentally disturbed, as long as the beliefs don't interfere with one's functioning or cause a significant emotional upheaval in other people. No one is an island, and what one believes and how one acts are going to be noticed and evaluated by one's family, friends, coworkers and acquaintances. Whether or not one's behavior is going to be seen as abnormal depends to a large extent on the tolerance of others and how rigid social norms are.

Voices from the Grave

Take the case of communicating with the dead. If someone told you he hears the voices of dead people and can communicate with them, what would you think? Is this within the norms of our society? Would it bother you to be around such a person? Would you think that the person was hallucinating and needed psychiatric or psychological treatment? If you considered hearing voices of dead people abnormal, you would probably want such a person to be treated to help them get rid of the voices. But it could be that you consider hearing from dead people possible and normal.

A living example is Rebecca Rosen, a thirty-three-year-old mother. Her grandmother committed suicide when Rebecca was eleven years old, and when Rebecca was in college she suddenly started hearing the voice of her dead grandmother. Her grandmother's voice provided guidance lessons for taking care of herself and avoiding depression and Rebecca wrote down all the things her dead grandmother told her. Since then she hasn't stopped hearing from other dead people, and continues to hear voices of the dead some ten years later.

Has Rebecca been treated as abnormal or mentally disturbed? No, she has been accepted as a psychic and she is booked almost three years in advance for psychic readings at $275 for a half-hour and $500 for an hour. In February 2010 she gave a group reading at the Rock Financial Center in Novi, Michigan, which was attended by eight hundred people who paid $30 to $80 apiece for readings. Rebecca says, "I think people are curious to know—have solid validation—that there is life after death and comforted to hear their deceased loved ones are okay and still with them."[2] Apparently believing in the supernatural is alive and well, and communicating with the dead is reassurance that there is life after death.

What is striking in this particular case is that Rebecca Rosen accepts hearing her dead grandmother's voice without worrying about whether she is having hallucinations and going off the deep end. How many people would be that casual about hearing the voice of a dead relative and accepting that they were actually in touch with the dead relative? Perhaps the lack of personal distress is an important factor in determining when a particular paranormal phenomenon is perceived as abnormal. After all, if people are comfortable with what is happening to them, they won't seek professional help and would avoid being diagnosed with a mental disorder.

What happens when people are distressed about being over-anxious, too compulsive, or having disturbing visions? They might then go to a mental health professional to get help. Such help can come from biofeedback procedures, or from some kind of talk therapy along with appropriate medication. You wouldn't expect a reputable psychiatrist, psychologist, or other mental health professional to use procedures based on the beliefs of psychics, mediums, or shamans, would you? Well, I certainly didn't, but the world is full of surprises.

Visions and Memories from a Past Life

I happened to be watching the "Oprah Winfrey Show" on May 13, 2008, when she introduced Dr. Brian Weiss, a psychiatrist now in private practice who was once chairman of the psychiatry department at Mount Sinai Hospital in Miami. He proceeded to hypnotize several people who were still suffering from anxiety and panic attacks after having undergone unsuccessful therapy with other mental health professionals. (Who these therapists were, what kind of therapies they practiced, and how long the clients saw them was a little fuzzy.)

While in a trance these subjects were regressed back to their childhood and then further back to "past lives." They then recalled who they had been in their past lives and some traumatic experiences they had undergone that had never been fully resolved. They talked about these traumatic experiences with much emotional candor, and when they came out of their trances they were convinced that these past-life experiences were the cause of their anxiety and panic disorders. They were also convinced that these disorders were now cured, since they laid bare how they had been emotionally affected by these traumas.

Dr. Weiss stated that he didn't believe that people had past lives when he first started hypnotic regression procedures but he now believes that people do have past lives and when they become aware of and face the past-life traumas they have endured, their symptoms are reduced or disappear. Weiss seems to believe that the spirits or souls of people live on when they die, and that others can connect with them. He's not too sure how these connections take place, but he is sure that they do take place. He now holds workshops all over the United States informing practitioners about the efficacy of hypnotic regression to join clients with their past lives and find the roots of their mental disorders.

While the United States has shown some interest in the idea of a past life, India has been a fertile ground for supernatural beliefs about past life and reincarnation for centuries. The *Times of India* recently ran a story about past-life regression therapy. The authors of the story make note of the fact that "in a predominantly Hindu country like India, the concept of a past life and karma is as ancient and accepted as time itself, and finds mention in the Upanishads and Patanjali's Yogasutra." (Teachings that go back centuries and deal with the nature of reality, the individual soul, the universal soul, and the transmigration of souls.) They go on to say that a television show run by hypnotherapist Dr. Trupti Jaylin, who uses past-life regression therapy, "has sent interest in past-life therapy soaring."

Dr. Jaylin apparently helped a woman who envisioned a body floating in front of her whenever she took a shower with her eyes shut. She tried taking a shower with her eyes wide open, but the sound of the running water filled her with dread. Then night after night she dreamed of being raped. Out of desperation she sought out Dr. Jaylin, who with regression therapy took her back to her past life, which turned out to be a tragic one. The woman saw her sister being raped and pushed to her death over a waterfall as she stayed hidden and frozen with fright. When her sister's body crashed to the ground, she leaped out of hiding to help her but was swept away by the thundering torrent. Once she relived these experiences she was finally able to take a shower with her eyes closed, and the rape dreams vanished.[3]

The implication of this story seems be that we are dealing with buried or repressed memories that have a profound effect on the person who carries these memories. How do these memories get into someone's brain? In order for a past life to connect with the present, the spirit or soul of the person of the past life would somehow have to enter the DNA of the egg or sperm combining to create the person being conceived anew. Then as the brain matures, the memories associated with this spirit or soul would have to work their way into the new person's memory cells of the brain, especially the hippocampus and cortex, where long-term memories are stored. Otherwise, how could an individual's personality and mental afflictions be influenced by a past life? If spirits and souls are floating around free, it seems that there would be a good chance of their getting into the wrong egg or sperm at conception and influencing the wrong person. It would be like dialing a telephone number at random and hoping to connect with a future mate. The chances here are worse than those of winning a lottery.

A telling experiment would be to take a group of individuals with several different mental disorders listed in DSM-IV, like anxiety disorder, agoraphobia, obsessive-compulsive disorder, or sexual aversion disorder, and instruct them to pretend that they have had past lives. Then tell them to imagine—using as wild an imagination as they would like—something that might have happened to them in their past lives that could have brought about their present mental disorders. Or, tell these subjects to make up a story about someone in a novel whose past-life experiences could have produced a mental disorder that they, the writers, were currently experiencing. It certainly would be interesting to see what stories they came up with. If the stories were imaginatively connected to a person's disorder, but without the element of belief attached to them, it would tell us that one does not need hypnotic regression to a past life in order for one's symbolic brain to come up with "past-life" stories. As stated previously, the element of belief is what distinguishes reality from fantasy. Once believed, a fantasy becomes reality. Wasn't this the case when Madoff Investment Securities LLC, operating a Ponzi scheme, had investors believing in great returns for their money? This turned out to be a seventeen-billion-dollar fantasy!

Battling the Evil within Us

In a previous chapter I pointed out that in ancient Egypt, physicians believed that diseases came from evil spirits that entered the body through the mouth, nose, and ears. They also believed that symptoms like tightness of the chest and labored breathing could be caused by malicious demons, who were blocking the channels that carried air, water, and blood to different parts of the body. To rid the body of these malicious demons, physicians (who were also priests) used religious and spiritual rituals much like the practice of exorcism. When we look back today at ancient Egypt, we say that the physicians had mistaken beliefs. Today we are more enlightened and employ the sciences of medicine and psychology to diagnose and treat physical and emotional disorders; we wouldn't accept the notion that people are possessed by demons or of evil spirits that create these disorders—would we?

The answer is that we would and do! For example, Father Vincent Lampert, who was ordained a priest in 1991, is the head priest at St. Francis and Clare parish in Greenwood, Indiana. He is one of twelve exorcists in America today having been trained by Italy's head exorcist in Rome, where he witnessed and assisted in about sixty exorcisms. He receives five to six calls a week from people who believe they are possessed. He states that before each exorcism he goes through a series of prayers and attends confession so that the devil will not be able to reach him. He maintains that exorcisms are only performed as a last resort after physical and mental disorders are ruled out. To determine whether an individual is really possessed, he uses at least four indicators, namely: an ability to speak languages one has not previously learned; inhuman strength; knowledge of the unknown (like secrets of the exorcist or others in the room); and an inexplicable aversion to holy places.[4]

While some churches are still convinced that demons and evil spirits can possess people, this belief is certainly not shared by professionally trained doctors in the mental-health field—or is it? Believe it or not, this belief is shared by some mental-health professionals. M. Scott Peck, an American psychiatrist who died in 2005, conducted exorcisms on two women he was convinced were demonically possessed after they didn't fit any psychiatric condition of which he was aware. He was considered a reputable psychiatrist, was medical director of the New Milford Hospital Mental Health Clinic, and maintained a private practice in New Milford, Connecticut. He wrote several books, but his first and best-known book, *The Road Less Traveled*, sold more than ten million copies and made his reputation. After researching the phenomenon of exorcism he concluded that the Christian concept of possession was a genuine phenomenon. He apparently tried to get the psychiatric community to add a definition of evil to the DSM-IV, but they wouldn't buy it.[5,6]

Another American psychiatrist, Richard E. Gallagher, is still alive and active as associate professor of clinical psychiatry at New York Medical College and on the faculty of the Columbia University Psychoanalytic Institute, as well as maintaining a private practice. While demonic possession is quite rare, he says, it does occur. He maintains that people who are demonically possessed have a distinct syndrome that is "simply inexplicable on psychiatric or medical grounds." This syndrome includes the ability to speak an unknown language, abnormal physical strength, hidden knowledge, hatred of the sacred, the ability to levitate, and the ability to go into a trance-like state "interrupted by the presence of what appears as an independent, intelligent entity (or entities), and the expressed desire of this intelligence not to leave the afflicted."

Gallagher points to a recent case of a woman he calls "Julia," who was referred to him after she approached her local clergy for help because she felt she was being attacked by a demon or by Satan himself. She was initially referred to an official priest-exorcist, who got in touch with and collaborated with Dr. Gallagher. After a thorough psychiatric evaluation Dr. Gallagher found her to be highly intelligent, quite logical, and "in no way psychotic." Though raised as a Catholic, Julia no longer practiced the faith and was even involved with satanic groups. When she went into one of her trances she would spout threats, taunts, and "scatological language, phrases like, 'leave her alone, you idiot, she's ours' or 'leave, you imbecile priest' and the tone of her voice differed markedly from Julia's own."

Gallagher decided that an exorcism was in order and Julia agreed. A team was assembled to assist, consisting of "several qualified mental-health personnel, at least four Catholic priests, a deacon and his wife, two nuns (both nurses, one psychiatric) and several lay volunteers." During the exorcism Julia went into a quiet trance-like state, but then sounds came out of her that resembled "loud growls and animal-like noises, which seemed to the group impossible for any human to mimic. At one point, the voices spoke in foreign languages, including recognizable Latin and Spanish. (Julia herself only speaks English, as she later verified to us.)" She also exhibited enormous strength, as it took the religious sisters and three others to hold her down. "Remarkably, for about 30 minutes, she actually levitated about half a foot in the air."

At the end of his report, Dr. Gallagher remarks, "The exorcisms were seen as helpful but have not yet resolved the matter of the possession. It should again be noted that Julia herself had no recollection at all of what occurred during the ceremonies." He goes on to say, "Contrary to what secular opinion falsely asserts, an objective medical view can confidently conclude that assaults by the devil, like genuine miracles, are rare but quite real scientific facts, verifiable to all who are not afraid to confront the truth."[7]

Another psychiatrist, Alan Sanderson, who is British, also believes in possession by spirits. He believes that spirit attachment is responsible for much illness and aberrant behavior and that bringing this to the attention of medical and other health professionals is really important for the wellbeing of humanity. In 1999 he founded the British Association for Spirit Release, which is now called the Spirit Release Foundation, of which he is the chair. Since his introduction into spirit release by a hypnotherapist in 1992, he has used spirit release with many hundreds of patients. He believes that most spirit entities that attach themselves to humans are spirits of people who have died, but he is also open to the idea of negative spirits in the form of demons attaching themselves to people.

Sanderson's therapeutic intervention of spirit release, "unlike exorcism, is a permissive and loving procedure." He provides as an example his treatment of a depressed woman thirty-three years of age who had four spirits attached to her creating depression, anxiety, headaches, and panic disorder. These four spirits were identified under hypnosis and released during two sessions. This created a dramatic improvement, and the woman has remained symptom-free for more than two years, according to Dr. Sanderson. He thinks the climate of opinion in psychiatry is changing toward greater acceptance of spiritual attachment or possession, as distinct from multiple personality disorder (now known as dissociative disorder) or psychosis.[8]

But I Saw It with My Own Eyes

Speaking strange languages, talking in a different voice, and expressing a hatred of the sacred are all conceivable traits of an emotionally disturbed person. But the ability to levitate contradicts the law of gravity and is impossible to reconcile with any known physical or mental condition. So if one believes in spirits, demons, or the devil possessing an individual, then one can conclude that the law of gravity doesn't apply to these non-material entities. Apparently they can produce levitation of the person they possess.

I don't believe the scientific and mental-health communities would accept the fact that an individual can levitate. Yet Dr. Gallagher stated in his report about Julia that for about thirty minutes she actually levitated about half a foot in the air. It is not easy to contradict a reputable psychiatrist who was involved in the exorcism and says he saw it with his own eyes. No one would (or should) accuse him of deliberately fabricating or stretching the truth in order to gain notoriety. So how does a nonbeliever explain what Dr. Gallagher says he saw with his own eyes? The explanation would have to be that he was misperceiving or experiencing an illusion. Could this be the case?

Sometimes You Can't Believe What You See

I contacted James Randi, the noted debunker of the paranormal, on March 18, 2010, told him about Dr. Gallagher's report, and asked him to explain levitation. He corrected me immediately, saying that I shouldn't ask him about levitation, since it doesn't exist; the question should be why do people believe in levitation. When I told him what Dr. Gallagher said he witnessed Randi replied without a moment's hesitation, that Gallagher experienced an illusion.

Who is James Randi, and how can he be so sure? To start with, Randi began performing magical feats when he dropped out of high school at age seventeen and became a professional stage magician and escapologist a few years later. He is now eighty-one years old. In 1956, at the age of twenty-eight, he appeared live on *The Today Show* and remained in a sealed metal coffin submerged in a hotel swimming pool for 104 minutes, breaking Harry Houdini's record of ninety-three minutes. In his forties he became interested in people who claim to have paranormal abilities, and he has kept busy exposing such claims as fraudulent or nonsense. He was a founding fellow of the Committee for Scientific Investigation of Claims of the Paranormal (CSICOP) and is founder of The James Randi Educational Foundation, which offers a prize of one million US dollars to anyone who can demonstrate a supernatural ability under agreed-upon scientific testing standards. So far no one has been able to claim the prize.[9]

Randi told me he has performed fake levitation presentations, and that people in the audience swear that he actually levitates the subjects. Afterward he tells the audience that no one levitated, and he said that people in the audience argue with him and tell him he is wrong, despite the fact that he was the one giving the performance. He said people believe what they think they see, even if it is an illusion. To back up Randi's contention that levitation is an illusion, one can go to YouTube on the Internet and watch videos that reveal how the illusion is performed. There are numerous tricks involved, but it looks very real. Like Randi's audience, you may want to argue with the performers, who claim that actual levitation does not occur.

Eyewitness Testimony of a Rape Victim

Just as eyewitness reports of supernatural events can be questionable, so can reports of unlawful or violent behavior. An emotionally devastating example was given on *60 Minutes* by correspondent Lesley Stahl, who reported the story of Jennifer Thompson.

When Jennifer was a college student in 1984, an intruder broke the light bulb near her back door, cut the phone lines, and broke into her off-campus apartment while she slept. Jennifer woke up, screamed, and then felt a knife blade at her throat. The intruder told her to shut up, or he would kill her. She offered him money, her car, her credit card, but she realized that his intention was to rape her. She decided there was nothing she could do but study him and provide information to the police that would put him in prison forever. So while he was raping her, she was intently studying his face. After about half an hour she tricked him into letting her go, promising to fix him a drink. As soon as she got up, she ran out the back door, and the rapist fled.

She reported the rape to the police and worked closely with the detective assigned to her case. She helped the police make a composite sketch, and three days after the rape she was shown a photo lineup. She took her time to study each photo carefully, then picked up one and said, "That's the man who raped me." When asked if she was sure, she replied in the affirmative. The suspect in the photograph was a man named Ronald Cotton. He was arrested and put in a physical lineup for Jennifer to review. She again picked Ronald Cotton and said she was "absolutely certain." Cotton was put on trial, and when Jennifer was asked if she recognized her rapist in the courtroom she called out, "Ronald Cotton," and pointed a finger at him. It took the jury just forty minutes to reach a guilty verdict.

Ronald Cotton was sentenced to life in prison plus fifty years and sent to North Carolina Central Prison. His lawyers were able to get him a new trial when a look-alike convict named Bobby Poole admitted to another prisoner that he raped Jennifer Thompson. When Poole was called to the witness stand, Jennifer felt very angry at the lawyers defending Ronald Cotton. She told Lesley Stahl, the *60 Minutes* reporter, "I thought, how dare you? How dare you question me? How dare you paint me as someone who could possibly have forgotten what my rapist looked like? I mean, the one person you would never forget. How dare you?" She denied that Bobby Poole looked like the man who had raped her, and Ronald Cotton was convicted again and this time given two life sentences.

Important Questions to Consider in Eyewitness Reports

Dr. Richard Gallagher was eyewitness to the levitation of a woman undergoing exorcism by him and his staff; Jennifer Thompson was eyewitness, up close, to the man who raped her. Both of them were considered competent, and questioning their eyewitness testimony is like questioning their integrity and their ability to know reality when they see it. Jennifer Thompson's response at the second trial of Ronald Cotton sums up her feelings to the questioning of what she saw and these feelings could easily be extended to Dr. Gallagher. If what Jennifer claimed she saw turned out to be untrue, what would the consequence be? She would be responsible for locking up a man for life. Certainly she was aware of this, and therefore she put her integrity on the line when she made such a positive identification.

How about Dr. Gallagher? What would the consequences be if what he saw turned out to be true? It would set back the physical sciences, and force them to start from scratch to explain this mysterious force that negates gravity and makes people levitate. As a man of science, Gallagher must have been aware of this when he reported that Julia had levitated for thirty minutes. In effect, the importance of both eyewitness testimonies is enormous and therefore they deserve to be put to the most stringent tests that humans can devise.

The Law and Eyewitness Testimony

In Dr. Gallaher's case one has to sum up the evidence for the existence of spirits, demons, and the devil as well as the validity of hypnosis as a detector of these entities in a person. I've used hypnosis in my professional practice and have taught hypnosis for the Extension Division of the University of California, Santa Barbara. Hypnosis has a great potential for tapping into the imagination, fantasies, and inventiveness of the human mind. This is especially true for individuals who are highly suggestible (about 15 percent of the population) and those who are desperately seeking solutions to their problems. The use of hypnosis to find demons in people and take them back to past lives is great drama but poor science.

Luckily, the law has a new tool that can dispute false eyewitness testimony: DNA evidence. In Jennifer's case there was on the shelves of the Burlington Police Department a rape kit, ten years old, but containing a fragment of a single sperm with viable DNA. It proved that Ronald Cotton was innocent and Bobby Poole was the rapist. Lesley Stahl further reported that DNA evidence has exonerated more than 230 men, mostly in sex crimes and murder cases, 75 percent of which involved faulty eyewitness testimony.[10]

The United States Department of Justice, realizing that innocent men have been falsely accused and convicted of crimes based on eyewitness testimony, convened a group of experts to report on the reliability of eyewitness identification. The report, called *Eyewitness Evidence: A Guide for Law Enforcement*, was finished in October 1999. Janet Reno, attorney general at the time, made a statement in introduction of the report as follows, "Even the most honest and objective person can make mistakes in recalling and interpreting a witnessed event; it is the nature of human memory." The report echoes what Janet Reno stated about eyewitness mistakes and provides this summary of their findings:

> The legal system has relied on the testimony of eyewitnesses nowhere more than in criminal cases. Although the evidence eyewitnesses provide can be tremendously helpful in developing leads, identifying criminals and exonerating the innocent, this evidence is not infallible. Even honest and well-meaning witnesses can make errors, such as identifying the wrong person or failing to identify the perpetrator of a crime.[11]

So, while we tend to believe what we see and what other people tell us they see, when the stakes are high and the outcome is critical the standard for accepting a belief should be based on a rigorous (and hopefully scientific) examination of the evidence in order to rule out possible mistaken beliefs. Fortunately, the life of an individual is usually not at stake when we claim what we have seen, so even if we are wrong no great harm results. When we claim supernatural beliefs like spirits, demons, voices of the dead, and the voice of God, the laws of the natural world keep functioning and are not dependent on our beliefs, so no harm is usually done unless the beliefs interfere with normal functioning.

The Struggle to Stay Rooted in Reality

We are bombarded by advertisements, political opinions, religious dogma, human miracles, and the findings of science. In addition to the vast number of these ideas, our symbolic brain can generate its own ideas; thus, deciding which ideas are believable and which ideas are questionable can be a difficult process. As a result, our minds are open to false beliefs, illusions, and even delusions, some of which have the potential to steer us in the wrong direction when we are confronted by challenges or threats.

Children, for example, have to wrestle with whether Superman, Santa Claus, and vampires actually exist or are just imaginary. They usually depend on older children or adults to help them decide, but sometimes they have to learn on their own. As mentioned earlier, when I was about six years old I was totally convinced that if you swore on the Bible and told a lie, God would kill you during the night. Well, one time when two of my friends and I were playing around we noticed a bad smell in the room. Jokingly we accused each other of having farted, but each of us denied having done the smelly deed. We knew one of us was lying, so we challenged each other to swear on the Bible and avow our innocence, which we did with trepidation. Because of my entrenched belief, I totally expected that one of us would be dead by morning. To my amazement we all survived. It was a profound lesson for me to learn. My belief about God was untrue, and this made me question whether God actually existed. This lesson still haunts me today.

Children are notorious for carrying around mistaken beliefs and finding out the hard way that their beliefs can be wrong. Yet their imaginations keep refueling their belief systems and their struggle between reality and fantasy is a continuous one. How about illusions? Are children more prone to experience illusions because of their unbridled imaginations? We all know that telling kids scary tales around a campfire can keep them on edge listening for noises most of the night. Illusions about monsters and creepy things are easy to trigger in children, and children carry these tales back to their friends when they get home.

One psychologist, Lisa Capps, from the University of California at Berkeley, believes that many illusions of safety that children carry around are beneficial for handling fear, anxiety, and depression. She calls these "protective illusions" and thinks they may also be essential for maintaining optimism in adults recovering from illness or trauma.[12] However, the illusion of invincibility can get people into a whole lot of trouble, just as it can for groups and nations.

Although we can still navigate both the natural and cultural worlds of reality even when our brain produces some illusions, can we do the same when we entertain delusions (false beliefs without an external cause)? We can, as long as the delusion is narrow and doesn't absorb our complete time and attention or can fit in with our occupation. For example, a person believes he was born to be a famous author or that he has exceptional knowledge about the thoughts of his company's CEO; or a college student believes that a famous movie star or celebrity is in love with her. These individuals can still function in our society.

Things can get out of hand, however, or land one in a psychiatric facility, if one believes he is Jesus Christ or the Jewish messiah. I happened to meet Bobby, who had such a belief, while I was working as a psychologist in the county psychiatric inpatient unit. While a patient himself, he was very convincing to the other patients, or at least no one wanted to challenge his conviction. Luckily, no other patient had the same delusion, so there was no potential for the clash between two imaginary messiahs.

Delusions can become dangerous to those who hold them, or to others around them, if they take on a paranoid quality, such as the belief that one is being followed, conspired against, or targeted by a secret agency. This can result in dangerous behavior as the deluded person tries to protect himself from harm. Even groups and nations can become paranoid about danger from others. They may justify their behavior by maintaining they are just being overcautious, but in the end it amounts to paranoia and delusional thinking.

The internment of Japanese citizens on the West Coast during World War II, the uncovering of supposed communists by the McCarthy oommittee, and the conviction that Iraq had weapons of mass destruction are three examples that come readily to mind. This is why the Southern Poverty Law Center keeps track of hate groups like the neo-Nazi and anti-immigrant vigilante groups that are paranoid and delusional about Jews and non-whites taking over and destroying society.[13]

The case of Ahmad Suradji of Indonesia is an extreme example of how delusional beliefs, triggered by a dream, resulted in the making of a serial killer. When captured and interrogated by the police, Suradji told them that he had a dream in 1988 in which his father's ghost told him to kill seventy women and drink their saliva so that he could become a mystic healer. He admitted killing forty-two women and girls over an eleven-year period, whose ages ranged from eleven to thirty. He buried his victims in a sugarcane plantation near his home, with their heads facing his house, which he believed would give him extra power. He was arrested in 1997 after bodies were discovered near his home. It appears that women came to him freely for spiritual advice or to make themselves richer or more beautiful, since he was considered to be a sorcerer. After being tried and found guilty, he was sentenced to death and executed by a firing squad in 2008.

What Stokes Our Super and Supernatural Imagination

When we are exposed to stories of rocks having spirits, people communicating with the dead, people recalling past lives, and illness resulting from possession by spirits and demons, we are inevitably put in the position of either believing in the existence of a mystical, spiritual, supernatural world beyond the realm of nature and natural laws, or believing that our symbolic brain creates such a mystical and supernatural world with our super imagination. My position is that the supernatural world is created by our super imagination provided by our symbolic brain. But as I have tried to show, this spiritual, supernatural world continues to exist in the minds of most people and can be a great source of inspiration and comfort to those who believe. It is only when it interferes with a person's functioning or leads to harmful acts that it becomes a problem.

Is the creation of and belief in a mystical, spiritual world a natural or acquired product of our symbolic brain? A recent article entitled "Brain Science, God Science: Why Religion Endures" by Michael McGuire, a psychiatrist, and Lionel Tiger, an anthropologist, tackled this question.[14] They remark: "A god or some equivalent is a product of the normal human brain. It is almost a neurological secretion." They hypothesize that the idea of an afterlife changed everything around, because "Suddenly, unexpectedly, vividly, and spontaneously, there was a solution to nothingness." So the strong human aversion to uncertainty and ambiguity was resolved by a belief in an afterlife. This, they maintain, ensures the continuation of the human belief in the mystical and supernatural, as claimed by religion. Their final sentence reads: "Like it or not, the brain will continue to secrete religion as long as life generates problems."

McGuire and Tiger's proposition is much like that of Dean Hamer, who wrote about *The God* Gene,[15] Steven Pinker, who authored *How the Mind Works*,[16] and Bruce Hood, who proposed that we have a built-in *Supersense*.[17] McGuire and Tiger propose that it is the problems encountered in life's journey that trigger this religious outpouring or "neurological secretion." This coincides with anthropologist Jacob Pandian's formulation that supernatural beings and powers have been created to cope with feelings of helplessness, encounters with suffering and injustice, and feelings of fear and anxiety associated with illness and death.[18]

On the other hand, there are many knowledgeable people who maintain that our belief in the spiritual side of life and its ramifications are natural and coincide with how the world operates. Spiritual expression, they maintain, whether manifesting itself in a god or gods, angels, spirits, or paradise, doesn't need to be kindled by the fear and anxiety that problems and suffering bring. For example, Joseph Campbell postulated that myths, legends, and magical activities are created to represent intense emotions that words alone cannot adequately express,[19] and J. Bolte Taylor concluded that spirituality is encoded in the right hemisphere of the human brain.[20] World-renowned psychiatrist Deepak Chopra echoes the theme of spirituality being built into human nature. He writes, for example, "As spiritual unfoldment becomes conscious, the circle of life acquires another dimension. Your sense of self expands with no end in sight."[21]

So, in opposition to the idea that the supernatural and spiritual were created to handle life's problems is the idea that the supernatural and spiritual are natural expressions of ourselves and our relation to the world. A third point of view is that both of the above ideas have merit. Which idea is most persuasive at any one time depends on the circumstances that confront us. When a tragedy occurs and we call upon God or spiritual figures for comfort, then the first idea is at the fore. When one is out in nature and sees its beauty and awesome power, the second idea becomes more relevant. Both ideas contain the realization that humans can and do go beyond themselves and their natural boundaries to find meaning in their lives. We seem to be pushed and pulled by our own makeup and the forces that society and nature subject us to. These forces will be further explored in the upcoming chapter.

CHAPTER VIII

Control, Power, and the Supernatural

The Amazing Innate Nature of Life

The programs that are built into our animal family members are breathtaking. One can't help but wonder how such astonishing feats can be purely instinctive. But from all indications and observations, that's what they are. They could almost be called supernatural. Here are some examples.

Female loggerhead turtles have been tracked swimming six thousand miles across the Pacific Ocean from Mexico to Japan at one mile per hour. It takes them over a year to complete the journey, which they have never made before. Although they need air to breathe, they are able to swim underwater for four to six hours. They weigh from 170 to 350 pounds and can measure more than three feet long.[1] How in the world do they know their final destination and which way to go without a map or a GPS device? Six thousand miles without getting lost, and ending up at their destination—quite amazing!

What kind of marvelous internal mechanisms do they have for reading directions underwater or on the water, and for telling them where to stop? They do this solo. Do they have built-in magnetic compasses or are they pulled by forces of which we are not yet aware? Is their destination stamped into their brains at birth? They can't go by land-marks that birds can use or follow star patterns. Thinking about their feat almost makes one believe in magical forces at work or turtle spirits leading them on.

Another mystifying migration is that of the mon-arch butterfly. North American monarch butterflies travel some three thousand miles from Canada to Mexico. Flying only by day and roosting at night, they cover fifty to one hundred miles per day, taking up to two months to complete the journey. Whereas the normal lifespan of a monarch butterfly is around a month, those that take part in the migration live from six to eight months. Fall migra-tion begins late August or early September and ends in the months of November and December. The same questions about the loggerhead turtle migration can be asked about the monarch migration. How do they know where they are going, and what built-in mechanisms steer them in the right direction?[2,3] If anyone is looking for supernatural-seeming feats, the migrations of the loggerhead turtles and the monarch butterflies seem like good candidates.

These examples demonstrate that built-in evolutionary programs can direct the behavior of animals, and natural selection is to thank for their persistence. This truism also applies to us humans. Even though we are conscious of much of our behavior and feel we can change it at will, the power of our innate nature frequently collides with our belief in free will. Addiction is an example of this collision, as are obsessions and compulsions. In this struggle between innate programming and free will we come face to face with our physical and emotional limits. Not liking limits, we are determined to go beyond them to as far a place as our imagination can take us. And take us far it does, to infinity and back, to the upper reaches of a world beyond our own.

Evolutionary Forces That Shape Our Lives

Although the debate between what is inborn and what is learned has been going on for centuries, there are many inborn forces that protect us from harm and help keep us alive. On the physical side, our biological immune system, which is an evolutionary gift, protects us against the multitude of pathogens we encounter daily. There is also a built-in psychological urge to protect, preserve, and enhance the life and physical well-being of ourselves and those we love, which pushes us to deal with both physical and emotional disorders. Medical and psychological sciences, which were born of this fight, have done wonders to help us, but spiritual or magical beliefs and practices can take priority when the sciences don't have all the answers.

A sobering example of this is presented in the book *The Horse Boy* by Rupert Isaacson. It provides a play-by-play account of how the author and his wife, Kristen Neff, struggled to find medical and psychological help in controlling the behavior of their son Rowan, who was diagnosed with an autistic disorder at age two.[4]

While this disorder finds a range of expressions in different children, the common elements are impairment and delay in social interactions, impairments in communication with others, stereotyped patterns of behavior, and delays in language and symbolic play.[5] Rowan showed impairments in many of these areas. He had difficulty making friends, his parents couldn't toilet train him, he was moody, and when he got upset over small things he would arch his back and scream bloody murder. He would retreat into himself for hours, shut off communication with his parents, and throw tantrums for no apparent reason at all. No matter what his parents tried, they couldn't seem to reach him or connect with him emotionally. Yet at times he would express his love for his parents and give them hugs, which is not the case with most autistic children. His parents tried going the medical route, but nothing seemed to help. They tried everything from yeast-free diets to behavioral therapy, but Rowan showed no improvement.

Rowan's mother, Kristin Neff, a psychology professor who specialized in child development and did research on self-compassion, felt very inadequate in dealing with Rowan's autism. In an interview she acknowledged how much grief she felt and that she loved Rowan so much she had a hard time admitting, "how difficult, how painful and how depressing it is sometimes." She continued, "I think autism breaks open your heart. The big lesson in life is that you can't control things, and you have to be open to what life brings you. You can bang your head against the wall of reality as much as you want and it won't help. Autism forces you to accept what you don't want."[6]

Rowan's father, a British journalist, author, and horse trainer, was also thrown by Rowan's autistic diagnosis. In his book he states: "The feeling was like being hit across the face with a baseball bat. Grief, shame—irrational shame as if I had cursed the child by giving him my faulty genes, condemned him to a lifetime of living as an alien."

He tried with all his might and savvy to deal with Rowan's constant distress, tantrums, incontinence, and social isolation, but, like his wife, he felt frustrated by not finding anything that worked.

The family lived near woods, and when Rowan went into the woods he became calmer. One day, when Rowan was about three, he ran into a neighbor's horse pasture and ended up in front of the neighbor's horse, Betsy. The horse dipped her head down low so Rowan could touch her. Isaacson, who knows horses, recounts his response to this scene: "I knew I was witnessing something extraordinary. The mare was spontaneously submitting to the child on the ground before her. In all the years that I had been train-ing horses, I had never seen this happen. My son had some kind of direct link to the horse."

After this experience Isaacson talked to his neighbor, who allowed him and Rowan to visit Betsy whenever they wanted. Rowan wanted to visit Betsy often, and being near her and touching her often calmed him down. His mother noticed that when Rowan was in the midst of a terrible tantrum, his father would put him on Betsy and he would calm down in an instant. There seemed to be a magical connection between Rowan and Betsy, which his father believed stemmed from some unexplainable, mystical connection between Rowan and horses. From his travels he knew that Mongolia was a place where the interaction between humans and horses was consid-ered sacred and where magical healing by shamans took place. He began to think that taking Rowan to Mongolia, putting him on horses, and allowing the shamans to use their powers on his son might do what the medical and psychological professions couldn't, and finally he made up his mind to give it a try. Although his wife was initially against the idea, she consented to go along. So when Rowan was five years old they all went to Mongolia to interact with the horses and the shamans.

They visited many shamans and underwent many magical rituals, which included the parents cleansing their private parts and submitting to a flogging, and the shamans running their fingers through Rowan's hair and over his body. They all rode horses across Mongolia, through prairies and swamps. In Mongolia, children like Rowan are treated as having spiritual leanings and many are schooled to become shamans, so the Mongolians included Rowan in their songs, dances, and trance rituals. His incontinence and tantrums stopped, and he began to interact with children his own age. He made many positive changes.

So here we have a sophisticated, educated couple who, when they couldn't find the answers they needed from modern medicine, went to seek answers from sources that relied on magical plus supernatural beliefs and practices. They were pushed by their built-in need to protect, preserve, and enhance the life and well-being of their son as well as their own well-being. While not all adventures into the magical and supernatural world turn out well, this one did. Here are the words of Rupert Isaacson: "The tantrums, the hyperactivity and anxiety—those ever-present demons that had squatted like gargoyles on Rowan's shoulders for the past three years—had left him completely by the time we'd been back in Texas a month. We had come back with a completely different child." They found control for Rowan's uncontrollable behavior in the world of the supernatural.

Another evolutionary force that shapes our lives can also be found in our closest living relatives, the chimpanzees, who protect their territory if necessary with their lives. This phenomenon is well documented by Jane Goodall, who lived among the chimpanzees in Gombe, Tanzania and wrote about her adventures in the book *Through a Window: My Thirty Years with the Chimpanzees of Gombe.*[7] A recent nine-year team study of chimpanzees in Uganda expanded the idea of territorial protection to include territorial invasion. John Mintani, the primatologist who led the team, sums up the study with these words: "The take-home message is quite clear and simple. Chimpanzees kill their neighbors to get more land." Experts have speculated that taking over the territory of others provides them access to more fruit trees and new females who live there.[8]

Strikingly similar tendencies to those of the chimpanzees can be witnessed in humans. The creation and demise of empires, kingdoms, and nations highlight the innate nature of humans to hold on to their own territory and to seize the territory of others when they get the chance to do so. World War II was fought over Hitler's determination to conquer and subjugate other nations; the first Iraq war was fought over Saddam Hussein's attempt to conquer and take over the oil fields of Kuwait; and after at least fifty years India and Pakistan have still not resolved their dispute over the territory of Kashmir.

We go a step beyond chimpanzees because of our symbolic brain, which allows us to designate property and possessions as precious, revered, sacred, and magical. When land becomes sacred because one's ancestors are buried there, the innate desire to hold on to the land becomes even stronger. This was the case when gold was discovered in the

Black Hills of the Dakota Territory in 1874 and prospectors started rushing in.

The Black Hills were sacred to the Lakota Indians; consequently, the Lakota defended the land but the US government was determined to move them to a reservation with the force of federal troops. The Lakota resisted, which resulted in the famous battle of Little Big Horn, where the Indians, under the leadership of chief Sitting Bull, defeated the Seventh Cavalry under the command of General George Armstrong Custer. This battle was, in fact, preceded by Sitting Bull's vision during a sun dance ritual, where prayers went to Wakan Tanka, their Great Spirit. Sitting Bull saw soldiers falling into the Lakota camp "like grasshoppers falling from the sky." Indeed, the attack by the Seventh Cavalry and its losses is seen by historians to pretty much follow Sitting Bull's vision.[9] Both prayers to Wakan Tanka and Sitting Bull's vision show how the supernatural can enter into defense of one's property.

While land can have sacred value, there are many other objects that we label as precious, divine, and hallowed. There are paintings worth millions of dollars, art objects and artifacts, writings and manuscripts, diamonds, gold, and many other glorified possessions that we feel duty-bound to protect, preserve, and enhance. Then there are objects that many believe have the power to protect humans because of the magical and supernatural qualities they possess. The Native American dream catcher, which is believed to have originated with the Ojibwa Chippewa tribe, is one example.

A Lakota story relates that Iktomi, the great trickster and searcher of wisdom, came in the form of a spider and spoke to an old Lakota spiritual leader in a sacred language. As the spider spoke, he picked up the elder's willow hoop with feathers, horsehair, and beads, attached and spun a web, and secured it to the hoop in a perfect circle with a hole in the center. Iktomi then told the spiritual leader that the web could be used to filter the good ideas and trap the bad ones, as long as one believed in the Great Spirit. So the story goes that the dream catcher lets only good dreams through and filters out bad ones, bringing the dreamer good luck and harmony.[10]

Other objects that have historically taken on magical and supernatural properties are wands, pendulums, stones, talismans, amulets, crystal beads, and swords. They have been and still are used for protection against illness, danger, misfortune, evil, and demons. They are also used to obtain profit, good fortune, love, happiness, and power. We have all heard of the crystal ball that can be used to foresee the future, and the Ouija board that is used to answer questions by magically directing the hands of the participants to letters and numbers.

The interesting part of the belief in objects having the powers to protect, heal, and bring happiness is that our belief itself actually does give these objects power. This is another reason why our symbolic brain has been favored by natural selection—the belief that objects are magical and powerful makes them magical and powerful and provides us with a sense of control over many different aspects of our lives.

A third evolutionary force that shapes our lives deals with disparaging remarks, insults, and disrespectful behavior from others toward you or your loved ones; this can create hurt, distress, anger, and a desire to retaliate. Complimentary remarks and respectful acts from others usually create feelings of appreciation, warmth, and a desire to respond in kind. In addition, there are also remarks from and behavior toward oneself. One can feel proud, ashamed, delighted, disgusted, amused, or angered toward oneself. People who are proud of and delighted with themselves tend to treat themselves well and take a positive approach to problems and challenges. People who are ashamed of or disgusted with themselves tend to treat themselves badly and look at problems and challenges in a negative way. They may also neglect to take care of themselves, and may even hurt themselves physically, like cutting themselves, or contemplate doing away with themselves.

I recall a well-respected professor, Alex H.— with whom I interacted on many occasions—who taught political science at a junior college and was very active in community affairs and politics. He prided himself in getting students involved in local causes, usually of a liberal nature, and presented very strong points of view on controversial local issues of student rights, minority rights, economic practices of the college district, and other socioeconomic issues.

Alex was a very ambitious, hard-driving person with very high expectations for himself and others. He pushed himself to succeed at all tasks, and seemed to need constant positive feedback from others about his accomplishments and his abilities. He used this feedback to allay his own doubts about himself, for he was always fighting against his fear of failure and constantly reminded himself that he failed to live up to his mother's expectation that he become a physician or a lawyer.

The college put on Alex's shoulders the job of teaching a brand-new course in urban affairs. He was worried about taking on this new responsibility and started having anxiety about his ability to teach the course at the level he expected of himself. He began to feel a lack of confidence; his anxiety level kept rising, and he started to feel panicky. He informed the college administration that he needed some time to prepare for such a course and took a leave of absence, which he hoped would help him regain his composure. Unfortunately, he chided himself for not having the strength to deal with his anxiety and was upset with himself for being so weak.

So, after a short leave, Alex went back to teach the course he feared. During the course his confidence waxed and waned, and he had to contend with frequent bouts of anxiety. Unable to handle the continued stress, he told the administration he wouldn't be able to finish teaching the course, and left in the middle of the semester. Seeing himself as a failure and believing his wife and children were ashamed of him, he made several suicide attempts and finally succeeded on his third try. Needless to say, his family was devastated, since they saw him as a warm, caring, and competent person.

While some may see Alex's suicide as a shameful and cowardly act, this characterization is disputed by Dr. Thomas Joiner, an expert on suicide. He maintains that "suicide requires a kind of courage or strength" to overcome the built-in urge to survive. He goes on to say that "so long as a person remains fearful of death and the actions and consequences of the activities that will create death, the actual act of suicide is unlikely." He says people have to work up to the act in a way that gets them more and more used to the pain and fear associated with self-harm, and they gradually lose their natural inhibitions against it. He maintains that when people become habituated to death and are no longer repulsed by it, "they can become attracted to it and can see it as a positive and beautiful thing."[11]

Perhaps this explains the mindset of Japanese suicide pilots in World War II, the followers of Jim Jones in Guyana, and the suicide bombers in Iraq and Afghanistan. This mindset can easily flow into belief in an afterlife, angels, paradise, heaven, meeting with deceased family members, and sitting in the house of God.

So while evolution has provided us with a brain that creates symbolic systems such as mathematics, language, and artistic expression, it has also created a conceptual image of ourselves that we continually evaluate for competency, worth, strength, likeability, and social status. As can be seen from Alex's example, this evaluation can have life-and-death consequences, depending upon the expectations of ourselves, how we handle adversity, and our spiritual connection to the world.

Conflicts among the Evolutionary Forces That Shape Our Lives

Since our brain is always symbolically primed, the conflicts that develop within ourselves and between ourselves and others have symbolic overtones. That's why the struggles within ourselves are often represented by battling forces and imaginary figures locked in battle. That's also why arguments over trivial subjects often represent much deeper antagonisms and become super-heated and emotionally volatile. In the midst of deep conflicts rationality can fly out the window, leaving us with only our emotional selves. Many of the myths and legends that have come down through the ages represent the same conflicts that engulf us today. Many of the supernatural figures represent the emotions that have emerged in these conflicts. In my book *The Psychological Immune System*, I identify and shed light on some of the conflicts I'm referring to.[12] It is my belief that these conflicts are universal in nature.

Life and Physical Well-Being versus Sense of Self and Identity

This conflict can also be depicted as self-preservation versus self-respect, death versus honor, body versus soul or physical self versus spiritual self. Persons in law enforcement, fire protection, and the armed forces must continually face this conflict, as their jobs require that they sometimes put their lives at risk and they never know when they might face death. When a situation arises that puts their lives and bodies in peril, they learn whether their oaths and commitment to their job can rise above their need to survive.

Facing death might be easier if they believe that angels are guarding them or that their souls live on and that heaven or paradise awaits. This conflict has been portrayed in stories of mythical heroes like Mwindo in Africa, King Arthur in Europe, and Rama in India. The great religious figures—Moses, Jesus, Mohammed, and Buddha—also faced this conflict as they risked their lives and tolerated great hardships for the sake of their spiritual convictions.[13]

Recognizing the difficulty of this conflict, countries around the world honor those individuals who have risked life and limb for their country. The highest military decoration awarded by the United States, created by President Lincoln in 1861, is the Medal of Honor for "gallantry and intrepidity at the risk of his or her life above and beyond the call of duty" while engaged in an action against an enemy of the United States.[14]

Gallantry and intrepidity certainly characterize the actions of Raymond Murphy as a second lieutenant and platoon commander of Company A during the Korean War. This is how his Medal of Honor citation reads:

> Although painfully wounded by fragments from an enemy mortar shell while leading his evacuation platoon in support of assault units attacking a cleverly concealed and well-entrenched hostile force occupying commanding ground, Second Lieutenant Murphy steadfastly refused medical aid and continued to lead his men up a hill through a withering barrage of hostile mortar and small arms fire, skillfully maneuvering his force from one position to the next and shouting words of encouragement. Undeterred by the increasing intense enemy fire, he immediately located casualties as they fell and made several trips up and down the fire-swept hill to direct evacuation teams to the wounded, personally carrying many of the stricken Marines to safety.[15]

One can sense in this account Raymond Murphy's intensity of focus in carrying out his duty without regard for his own safety. Whether due to loyalty to country, concern for the men in his platoon, or a spiritual mindset, he was willing to risk his life. While some animals will fight to the death to protect their offspring or their hierarchical position and territory, only the human animal is able to give up his life for a personal, social, or spiritual cause.

The citation explains why the medal was given to Raymond Murphy, but the medal stands alone as a symbol for his actions and represents his inner strength of purpose. Most nations also have medals for their soldiers who show exceptional valor. France has La Legion d'Honneur (National Order of the Legion of Honour), Britain has the Victoria Cross, China issues the War Memorial Medal, and Pakistan gives out the Emblem of Haider (Haider is the epithet of Hazrat Ali and means "Lion").[16]

The conflict between one's life and one's self-respect also emerged quite unexpectedly and profoundly when Uruguayan Air Force Flight 571, carrying a rugby team and their families from Uruguay to a match in Chile, crash-landed in a desolate glacial valley in the Andes. Fifteen people died, including the pilot; five were badly injured; but miraculously twenty-nine survived with minor injuries. Their hope of being rescued stretched from hours, to days, to months, and was dashed by news on their makeshift radio that the search for them had been called off. The cold and raw conditions resulted in more deaths, until the number of survivors was down to sixteen. The dead were buried in the snow and rocks with as much dignity and reverence as could be mustered.

With starvation staring them in the face, the last sixteen survivors decided that they had to choose their lives over their moral revulsion at eating the flesh of their teammates and family members, so they did and managed to survive. A film was eventually made of their ordeal, which brought out how painful the decision was to cannibalize their comrades. Thirty years later, each man still wrestles with this act. As one of the survivors stated, "We all found it hard. What we were doing was unthinkable. But I made up my mind. I chose to live." The team's captain urged his fellow players to think of this necessary sacrilege as "holy communion" and insisted that by doing what they did they were keeping part of the others within themselves. From the crash to their rescue was a seventy-two-day odyssey.[17]

While these stories are very dramatic and intense, the same conflict goes on in the lives of everyone. End-of-life issues, including doctor-assisted suicide, stand as very relevant twenty-first-century considerations. Also, think of a time when you took a risk involving your life or physical well-being and the motivation that made you take this risk.

Many sports involve the risk of injury, yet people continue to engage in them despite the risk. Many people skydive, scuba dive, rock climb, or mountain climb for the thrill of accomplishment and personal satisfaction. These activities continue because humans also have the need to enhance their sense of self, and his need can be more powerful than the need to protect one's physical well-being.

Heightened danger itself can even act as an incentive to take greater and greater risks. People talk about the adrenaline rush that pushes them to go beyond themselves. This has the potential to cause one's symbolic brain to imagine human invincibility and grasp the spiritual and supernatural aspects of the world. We create medals, stories, movies, and myths to back up these feelings and beliefs. The almost fanatical interest in vampire and Harry Potter movies, which are steeped in supernatural themes, plays on these beliefs and on our desire for superhuman powers.

Life and Physical Well-Being of Oneself versus Life and Physical Well-Being of Others

This conflict manifests itself in both real and symbolic terms when two boxers, martial-art experts, or wrestlers get into a ring to battle each other. These sports, especially boxing (fist-fighting) and wrestling, go back thousands of years and were practiced by ancient Egyptians, Greeks, and Romans. Cave drawings going back fifteen thousand years depict wrestling holds that are still used today, and images of men getting ready to fist-fight have been found on stone tablets believed to be seven thousand years old.[18,19] It seems that humans have an innate urge to challenge each other physically, a trait also found in other predatory animals.

While men are the main challengers, in modern times more and more women have taken an interest in the arts of physical combat. In today's competitive culture it seems that girls are willing to fist-fight, when physically intimidated, just as readily as boys. It was recently reported that an argument between two girls at a local high school escalated into a fist fight when one girl pushed the other. The fight resulted in an injury to one of the girls. Fights also break out when bullied students decide to fight back, and some resort to using weapons like guns and knives. Such fights can quickly escalate into matters of life and death.

This conflict is readily resolved when someone is seen as a threat to oneself, one's family, or the groups one identifies with. When people can be labeled as enemies, evil, or hostile, it is not difficult to choose one's own life or well-being over theirs. But difficulties arise when the other is not considered an enemy, evil, or hostile. In that case, how much risk is a person willing to take to protect the life or well-being of someone else? If that someone else is family or a friend, the amount of danger one is willing to face is probably a lot higher than if they were strangers. You see someone being accosted on the street by another; what do you do?

A situation similar to this occurred when a man, M.H., with his fiancée, were getting on the freeway and saw a woman with a knife chasing a man around a parked truck. What did he do? Did he call 911 and wait for the police to come? No, he stopped his car, got out, and grabbed the woman's arms. Even though she bit his wrist he did not let go, because he was afraid she would kill the man she was chasing. His fiancée called 911 but also got out to help, and pulled the woman's feet out from under her. M.H. eventually pinned the woman to the ground and waited for the police to come. The male victim had been stabbed more than twenty times and suffered a punctured lung. The police stated that M.H. had saved the victim's life.[20] Not everyone is willing to risk his life to save the life of a stranger. The victim was lucky M.H. was that kind of person.

Another story involving two brothers brings out the willingness of one brother to risk his life without hesitation for the life of the other. It seems that ten-year-old Tim had ventured onto the ice in their backyard pond to see if it was safe to skate on. He made it across the pond, but on his way back the ice broke apart and he fell through and became trapped. Realizing what had happened, his nineteen-year-old brother, Jay, dove into the icy pond in an effort to rescue Tim. Unfortunately both brothers became trapped and both died. When the police were called it took rescuers three hours to locate the brothers under twelve feet of water. This example of one family member risking his life for that of another family member could probably extend to practically every family in existence. Natural selection looks favorably on strong family bonds, because this helps to preserve the lives of each member and the family, which is the basic unit of society.

Not only do people challenge each other and pit their lives against the lives of others, but so do groups and nations who expect their members to risk their breath and bodies for their preservation. This goes for groups as small as gangs, even groups as paranoid as the Aryan Nations and as destructive as Al Qaeda. Of course, when groups or nations do battle with each other, it's the individual members who do the fighting and dying.

Loyalty is at the root of an individual's willingness to risk life and limb for his group or country. Once fighting has begun it is almost impossible to stop unless the top leadership is willing to call a truce. However, on the first Christmas Day of World War I, British and German troops allowed the spirit and rituals of Christmas to intercede in their fighting. German troops lit candles on Christmas trees so British sentries a few hundred yards away could see them, and British troops lit bonfires and sent up rocket flares in response. Each side understood these signals to mean a truce was desired so that the spirit of Christmas could be celebrated. British and German soldiers came out of their trenches to greet each other and exchanged gifts of tobacco, jam, sausage, chocolate, and liquor. Needless to say, the generals were shocked and high command diaries and official reports expressed fear that this sort of interaction could diminish the troops' willingness to fight. And although a German army order named fraternization as high treason, no soldier was punished for this Christmas truce. After this, at the insistence and threat of the high command, the war really began in January 1915, eventually claiming ten million lives.

So, while the conflict between one's life and the life of another may be better resolved by the bottom players in a group, the outcome in a structured group ultimately depends on the decision of the leaders who hold the power.

Do humans need to challenge, compete with, and fight each other? Is this built into the human genetic makeup? It sure seems that way, and the symbolic expression of this conflict can be found in myths and legends going back to ancient Egypt and Greece. In ancient Egypt, for example, the battle between the gods Horus and Set is well documented throughout Egyptian mythology, as is the battle between Zeus and his father, Cronus, in Greek mythology.[22,23] Life-and-death conflicts between individuals, between groups, and between nations have been going on since recorded history began and are still taking place in the twenty-first century. These conflicts must sometimes feel as if they have reached supernatural proportions, and the leaders in power must feel they are godlike, akin to the Pharaohs in ancient Egypt.

The Effect of Control and Power on Our Symbolic Brain

As humans we rely on control and power to protect, preserve, and enhance our lives, possessions, and identity. In the natural world we try to control the flow of rivers by building dams, the growth of forests by cutting down and planting trees, livestock predation by trapping or killing wolves and bears, the preservation of certain species by placing them on the endangered species list, and the pollution of rivers, lakes, and oceans by regulating the amount of waste flowing into them.

In our man-made world we try to control almost everything: what we produce and how it's distributed, the safety of the cars we drive and the rules of the road, the cleanliness of our drinking water, the economic balance between supply and demand, the role fairness and justice should play in our societies, and the education systems we expose our children to. We try to get people, starting with young children, to control their bowel movements, their temper, their aggressiveness, their desires (for food, sex, money, and special consideration), their exploitation of others, and their tolerance for differences among people. We all feel less anxious and more at ease when we sense that things are under control. When people break the rules of society, act out against others, or cannot contain their emotions, we instinctively say they are out of control. Programs for people who are out of control have self-control as their direction and goal.

The desire for control and power pushes our symbolic brain to develop models and belief systems about how things work and ways to use these models and belief systems to create programs, principles, and products to achieve the results we desire. Sometimes our models and beliefs are saturated more with our wishes, fears, and imaginary visions than with facts that can enhance our survival. This dichotomy is continually played out in our lives via the communications media that we are all exposed to. Sometimes it's hard to discern what is real and what is imaginary. And it is difficult to predict how people will react when they experience changes in power and control.

An interesting and informative experiment done by psychologist Dr. Phillip Zimbardo with his freshman class at Stanford University shows the effects of one group gaining power over another. Volunteers, who tested as emotionally stable, were randomly divided into prisoners and guards and were instructed to play their roles as best they could in a two-week experiment. They improvised a jail setup in the basement of the psychology building and devised rules about treatment and punishment. The guards were given authority to control the behavior and activities of the prisoners by withholding privileges and instituting non-physical punishment like doing pushups and being isolated in a dark closet. They could also wake up the prisoners at any hour—like three a.m.—for inspection.

A rebellion by the prisoners on the second day was quelled with the use of fire extinguishers, and as punishment the prisoners' mattresses were removed so they had to sleep on the concrete floor. By the fourth day the guards were taking more and more control of the prisoners, and both callous and sadistic behavior started to emerge. Some of the prisoners showed signs of erratic, emotionally unstable, and depressive behavior. Things got so bad that the experiment had to be halted after six days in order to preserve the mental health of the students who took on the role of prisoners.

When the experiment ended and the students had a chance to review the results, many of the students who played the guards were quite surprised at how callous and controlling they had become because of the power they had been given.[24]

Something very similar occurred at the third-grade level when teacher Jane Elliot designed an experiment to show her students how prejudice felt.[25] On the first day of the experiment she arbitrarily designated brown-eyed children as superior to blue-eyed children to see what results would ensue. The brown-eyed children lorded it over the blue-eyed children; they mistreated their former friends, got into fights with them, and informed school officials that the blue-eyed children might be stealing things. On day two Ms. Elliot informed her class that she had made a big mistake and that it was blue-eyed students who were superior to brown-eyed students. The same type of behavior resulted as on day one only in reverse: now the blue-eyed children lorded it over the brown-eyed class members. This experiment, like the Stanford one, shows that when authority is given to one group over another the group in authority uses its power to control the second group. It might be better to say that the group in authority misuses its power to control the less-powerful group.

In actuality, since groups are made up of many individuals, the authority and power of the group are felt and absorbed by the group members.

So individuals in the authority group are really using their power to exert control over individuals in another group. Gaining power seems to change the mindset and actions of people to become more aggressive and to exert more control over the actions of others less powerful.

Supernatural Beliefs in Relation to Control and Power

Let's review some of the stories and examples already given about supernatural beliefs and look at how they relate to control and power.

1) **Belief in supernatural powers to control physical and emotional disorders**. This was exemplified in the story of *The Horse Boy*, where shamans were used to control autism; in the story in which psychiatrists regressed clients back to their past lives to control anxiety and panic disorders; and in accounts of both priests and psychiatrists using exorcism to cast out the invading demons who caused mental disorders. Faith healing also falls into this category.

2) **Belief in the supernatural to control emotional pain resulting from the loss of loved ones**. This use of the supernatural was highlighted in Rebecca Rosen's alleged ability to communicate with a person's dead relatives and the widespread belief in India about reincarnation. It also coincides with the belief in an afterlife, going to heaven or paradise, and prayer to reach departed souls. As long as one believes that death is not a permanent state, that the dead live on and can be reached now or later, then the heartbreak of death loses much of its sting. The intensity of emotional pain is controlled.

3) **Belief in a connection with supernatural powers that protect one's community and property, control future events, and work in harmony with nature.** The Eveny people of Siberia described in Chapter IV are excellent representatives of a people who are immersed in the supernatural and who use it to help them cope with their harsh climate, rugged natural environment, and unpredictable future. They believe that spirits occupy rocks, fire and weapons; that the way fire burns can direct them to their lost reindeer; and that their shamans have the power to look into the future. On a less solemn level, we have seen that crap-shooters use magical beliefs and rituals to control the dice and overcome the randomness of probability. This extends to the superstitious habits of athletes and gamblers who use talismans and ritualized gestures to try to control unpredictable outcomes.

4) **Belief in a divine spirit or spiritual powers that can be tapped into because they actually reside in the human makeup and the human psyche.** Joseph Campbell postulated that myths and magical rituals actually represent intense feelings and emotions that normal language fails to handle, and Deepak Chopra believes that consciousness of our spirituality provides us with power and control over ourselves and our interactions with nature. Jill Bolte Taylor is convinced that spirituality is built into the right hemisphere of the brain; Dean Hamer informed us about the God Gene; and Bruce Hood concluded that supernatural beliefs are held by all children and that adult supernatural beliefs result from childhood misconceptions that have not been disposed of. So, this type of spirituality and supernaturalism has the potential to look at the power and control within ourselves, acknowledge

the power of others, and see ourselves as something special and beyond our physical makeup.

Concluding Remarks

The implication of the above four categories is that we create supernatural beliefs consciously or unconsciously to help us adapt to physical and psychological adversity, the social world we live in, and the natural world around us. These beliefs also represent our intense human emotions and our conviction that we are special and more than our physical selves. What is more than the physical self we designate as the spiritual self, a self that doesn't conform to the laws of science as we know them and that is based on faith that can be passed down from generation to generation.

To generate these supernatural beliefs we need and have been endowed with a symbolic brain. It took evolution three and a half billion years to produce an animal that can understand a non-symbolic world in symbolic terms. We are that animal. Fortunately, we have developed beliefs about ourselves and the world with the benefit of science based on repeatable observation, experimentation, logical proof and model creation. And while it is true that false models and false beliefs can lead to disastrous consequences, supernatural beliefs continue to exist because they actually do serve human survival by reducing anxiety, fear, stress, and the feeling of alienation. Our symbolic brain's penchant for the supernatural is a mixed blessing—but a blessing, surely, nevertheless.

REFERENCES

Chapter I

1. Graceffo, Antonio (2007). The Sea Gypsies of Surin Island. *Asia Sentinel*, 7/25/08, 1:54. http://asiasentinel.com
2. The University of Albany, Science Library (2007). Dialogs with Bacteria: Quorum Sensing. 1/9/07, 9:49. http://library.albany.edu/science/newinsci_quormsensing.htm
3. Gibbs, K., M. Urbanoriski, and P. Greenberg. (2007). Genetic Determinants of Self Identity and Social Recognition in Bacteria. *Science*, 321:256
4. Shirber, Michael (2005). Ants Rely on Chemicals to I.D. Enemies. *Science*, 6/9/05. http://www.livesciences.com
5. Webster, Bayard (1981). Smithsonian Uncovers Intricate Relationships Among Ants in the World. *The New York Times (Science section)*, May 26.
6. Kagan, Herman (2006). The Psychological Immune System: *A New Look at Protection and Survival*. Bloomington, Ind.: AuthorHouse.
7. Zimbardo, Philip G. (1992). *Psychology and Life* (Thirteenth Edition). New York: HarperCollins. 306.
8. Watson, John B. (1924). *Behaviorism*. New York: Norton.

9. American Psychiatric Association (2005). *Diagnostic Criteria from DSM-IV.* Washington, D.C. 207-208.
10. Brechbuhl, J., M. Klaey, and M-C Broillet, (2008). Gueneberg Ganglion Cells Mediate Alarm Pheromone Detection in Mice. *Science,* 321:1092.
11. Vitebsky, Piers (2005). *The Reindeer People.* New York: Houghton Mifflin.
12. Overall, Karen L. (2001). How Animals Perceive the World: Non-Verbal Signaling. Atlanta Coast Veterinary Conference. www.vin.com/VINDBPub/SearchPB/Proceedings/PRO5000/PRO6378.htm
13. *National Geographic Complete Birds of the World* (2009). Tim Harris,Ed., Washington, D.C.: National Geographic Society
14. DeWaal, Frans, B.M. (1995). Bonobo Sex and Society: The Behavior of a Close Relative Challenges Assumptions about Male Supremacy in Human Evolution. *Scientific American,* 272:82.

REFERENCES

CHAPTER II

1. Keller, Helen (1904). *The Story of My Life.* New York: The Century Company. 7-8. http://digital. library.upenn.edu/women/Keller/life/Part-1
2. Vietnam Library Network (2008). Feb.08. http:// www. Vietnamlibrary.net
3. *World Book* (2001). Mac OSX Edition. World Book, Inc.
4. Roffwarg, H.P., et al. (1966). Ontogenetic Development of the Human Sleep-Dream Cycle. *Scienc*e 152:604.
5. Ibid.
6. Hurovitz, Craigs, et al. (1999). The Dreams of Blind Men and Women: A Replication and Extension of Previous Findings. *Dreaming*, 9:183-193.
7. Greenspan, S. and Greenspan, N.I. (1985). *First Feelings: Milestones in the Emotional Development of Your Baby and Child.* New York: Viking Penguin, Inc., 143.
8. Caird, R. (1994). *Ape Man: The Story of Human Evolution.* New York: MacMillan.
9. Kagan, Herman (2006). *The Psychological Immune System: A New Look at Protection and Survival.* Bloomington, Ind.: AuthorHouse
10. Goodall, Jane (1990). *Through a Window: My Thirty Years with the Chimpanzees of Gombe.* Boston: Houghton Mifflin Co.

11. Snibbe, Alana C. (2004). Taking the 'VS' Out of Nature vs. Nurture. *The APA Monitor* 35 (10):22. 182
12. Johanson, Donald and Blake, Edgar (1996). *From Lucy to Language.* New York: Simon & Schuster.
13. Davies, Glyn (2002). *A History of Money from Ancient Times to the Present Day.* (Third edition). Cardiff: University of Wales Press.
14. Weatherford, Jack (1994). *Savages and Civilization.* New York: Crown Books.
15. DeWaal, Fran B.M. (1992). The Chimpanzee's Sense of Social Regularity and Its Relation to the Human Sense of Justice. *The Sense of Justice: Biological Foundations of Law.* Roger D. Masters & Margaret Gruter, eds. Newbury Park, Calif,: Sage Publications. 241.

REFERENCES

CHAPTER III

1. Lown, Bernard (1996). *The Lost Art of Healing.* New York: The Ballantine Publishing Group. 31.
2. Saks, Elyn R. (2007). *The Center Cannot Hold.* New York: Hyperion. 182.
3. Weil, Andrew (1995). *Spontaneous Healing.* New York: Fawcett Columbine. 71.
4. Bownds, M. Deric (1999). *The Biology of Mind: Origins and Structure of Mind, Brain and Consciousness.* New York: John Wiley & Sons. 259.
5. Duin, Nancy, and Suttcliffe, Jenny (1992). *History of Medicine.* New York: Barnes & Noble Books. 191.
6. Cousins, Norman (1979). *Anatomy of an Illness as Perceived by the Patient.* New York: W.W. Norton & Co. 69.
7. Zubieta, Jon-Kar et al. (2005). Brain's Painkillers May Cause 'Placebo Effect.' *Journal of Neuroscience*, 25:34.
8. Diederich, N.J., and C. G. Goetz (2008). The Placebo Treatments in Neurosciences: New Insights from Clinical and Neuroimaging Studies. Neurology 71:677.
9. Lown, Bernard (1996). Healing (see #1).29

10. Zubieta, Hoh et al. (2008). Placebo and Nacebo Effects Are Defined by Opposite Opioid and Dopaminergic Responses. *Archive of General Psychiatry* (2).220-231

11. Sapolsky, Robert M. (2005). The Influence of Social Hierarchy on Primate Health. *Science,* 308:648

12. Kagan, Herman (2006). *The Psychological Immune System: A New Look at Protection and Survival.* Bloomington, Ind.: AuthorHouse.

13. Pelletier, Kenneth R. (1993). Between Mind and Body: Stress, Emotions, and Health. *Mind Body Medicine.* Daniel Goleman & Joel Gurin, eds. New York: Consumer Reports Books. 35-38.

14. Selye, Hans (1974). *Stress without Distress.* New York: Harper and Row.

15. Shwartz, Mark (2007). Robert Sapolsky Discusses Physiological Effects of Stress. *Stanford Report,* March 7. http://news-service.stanford.edu/news/2007/march7/sapolsky-0307707.html.

16. Spiegel, David (1993). Social Support:How Friends,Family and Groups Can Help. *Mind Body Medicine. Daniel Coleman and* Joel Gurin, eds. New York: Consumer Reports Books. 331

17. Seligman, M.E.P., and Maier, S.F. (1967). Failure to Escape Traumatic Shock. *Jrl Exper Psych,* 74, 1

18. Abraham, L.Y., M.E.R Seligman and J.D.Teasdale (1978). Learned Helplessness in Humans. Critique and Reformulation. *Journal of Abnormal Psychology* 87, 49-74.

19. Seligman, M.E.P. (1991). *Learned Optimism.* New York: Alfred A.Knopf. 221.

20. Henslin, James M. (1967). Craps and Magic. *American Journal of Sociology,* 73:326.

REFERENCES

CHAPTER IV

1. Vitebsky, Piers (2005). *The Reindeer People: Living With Animals and Spirits in Siberia.* New York: Houghton Mifflin Co.
2. Kagan, Herman (2006). *The Psychological Immune System: A New Look at Protection and Survival.* Bloomington, Ind. AuthorHouse.
3. Pinker, Steven (1997). *How the Mind Works.* New York: W.W. Norton & Co. 554-65.
4. Campbell, Joseph (1988). *The Power of Myth. A Conversation between Bill Moyers and Joseph Campbell in 1985 and 1986,* Betty Sue Flowers, ed. New York: Doubleday. 45.
5. Pandian, Jacob (2001). The Dangerous Quest for Cooperation between Science and Religion. *SkepticalInquirer,* 25-5.28.
6. Hamer, Dean (2004). *The God Gene: How Faith Is Hardwired into Our Genes.* New York: Anchor Books. 8.
7. Taylor, J. Bolte (2008). *My Stroke of Insight: A Brain Scientist's Personal Journey.* New York: Viking Books. 41.
8. Weil, Andrew (1995). *Spontaneous Healing.* New York: Fawcett Columbine. 71.

9. Sutcliffe, Jenny, and Duin, Nancy (1992). *A History of Medicine*. New York: Barnes & Noble Books. 14.
10. Bach, Marcus (1961). *Strange Sects and Curious Cults*. New York: Dorset Press.

REFERENCES

CHAPTER V

1. Kagan, Herman (2006). *The Psychological Immune System: A New Look at Protection and Survival.* Bloomington, Ind.: AuthorHouse.
2. Massie, Barry M., and Amidon, Thomas A. (1997). Heart. *Current Medical Diagnosis and Treatment* (36th Edition). Lawrence M. Tierney, Jr., et al., eds. Stanford, CT: Appleton & Lange.
3. Wikipedia (2010). Ancient Egyptian Medicine. http://en.wikipedia.org/wiki/Ancient_Egyptian_Medicine.
4. Arab, Sameh M.(2010). *Medicine in Ancient Egypt.* Arab World Books. http://www.arabworldbooks.com/articles8.htm
5. Shaw, Ian (2000). *The Oxford History of Ancient Egypt.* Oxford: Oxford University Press.
6. Stauffer, John L. (1997). Lung: Pleuropulmonary Infections. *Current Medical Diagnosis and Treatment* (36th edition). Lawrence M. Tierney Jr., et al. eds. Stanford, CT: Appleton & Lange.
7. Sutcliffe, J., and Duin, N. (1992). *A History of Medicine: From Prehistory to the Year 2020.* New York: Barnes & Noble Books. 14.
8. Wikipedia (2011). Bloodletting. http//en.wikipedia.org/wiki/Blood_letting.
9. Schulman, Bruce (2008). Medicine in Ancient Greece—Overview. *Learn, NC.* The University of North Carolina School of Education.

10. Lahanas, Michael. Examples of Ancient Greek Medical Knowledge. www.mlahanas.de/Greeks/med/htm.
11. Sutcliffe & Duin (1992). *History Medicine.* (see # 7) 16.
12. Lyons, Albert S. (2007). Medical History of Ancient China. *Health Guidance. www.health-guidance.*org.
13. Lyons, Albert S. (2009). Medical History of Ancient India. *Health Guidance. www.health-guidance.*org.
14. Sutcliffe and Duin (1992). *History Medicine.* (see #7) 17.
15. Indianetzone: Naturopathy (2009). Treatment of Common Fever in Ayurveda. www.indianetzone.com/treatment_common_ fever_ayurveda.htm.
16. Bownds, Deric (1999). T*he Biology of Mind: Origins and Structure of Mind, Brain and Consciousness.* New York: John Wiley & Sons.

REFERENCES

CHAPTER VI

1. Asimov, Isaac (1989). *Asimov's Chronology of Science and Discovery*. New York: Harper & Row. 341.
2. Lofholm, Nancy (2001). Prayed-Over Girl Died of Untreated Diabetes. *Denver Post Western Slope Bureau*. Feb. 8. www.rickross.com/reference/firstbornfirstborn8.html.
3. Caroll, Robert T. (2003). *The Skeptic's Dictionary. A Collection of Strange Beliefs, Amusing Deceptions and Dangerous Delusions*. New York: Wiley & Sons.
4. Asser, Seth M., and Swan, Rita (1998). Child Fatalities from Religion-Motivated Medical Neglect. *Pediatrics*, 104-4. 625-29.
5. Kagan, Herman (2006). *The Psychological Immune System: A New Look at Protection and Survival*. Bloomington, Ind.: AuthorHouse.
6. Basham, A.L. (1997). Hinduism. *Encyclopedia of the World Religions*. R.C. Zaehner, ed. New York: Barnes & Noble Books.
7. Degani, Meir H. (1963). *Astronomy Made Simple*. New York: Doubleday & Co.
8. Anonymous, (2001). Astrology. *World Book Multimedia Encyclopedia*. Mac OSX Edition. World Book Inc.
9. Wadler, Joyce, et al. (1988). The President's Astrologers. *People*, May 23, 29:20.

10. American Museum of Natural History (2001). *Cosmic Horizons: Astronomy at the Cutting Edge.* eds. Steven Soter and Neil de Grasse Tyson, New York: The New Press.
11. Ball, Timothy (2007). Global Warming: The Cold Hard Facts? *Canada Free Press,* Feb. 6. www.canadafreepress.com/2007/global-warming 020507.htm.
12. Bellamy, David (2008). BBC Shunned Me for Denying Climate Change. *Daily Express,* Nov.5.www.dailyexpress.co.uk/posts/view/69623.
13. Letter to Congress on Climate Change from 18 Scientific Societies. Oct. 21, 2009. www.aaas. org/go/climate_letter.
14. Hood, Bruce M. (2009). *Supersense: Why We Believe in the Unbelievable.* New York: HarperCollins. 97.
15. Vitebsky, Piers (2005). *The Reindeer People.* New York: Houghton Mifflin.

REFERENCES

CHAPTER VII

1. *Diagnostic Criteria from DSM-IV* (1994). American Psychiatric Association. Washington, D.C.
2. Montemuni, Patricia (2010). Supernatural Chic: Medium Rebecca Rosen Part of a White-Hot Trend. *Detroit Free Press*, Feb. 8.
3. Sucharita, Swati, and Ganesan-Ram, Sharmila (2010). A Peek into Your Past Life. *The Times of India*, Feb. 14, 1-2.
4. Palmer, Katie (2009). Exorcist Shares Past Experience with Demonic Possession. *The Daily Illini*, Oct. 28.
5. Wikipedia (2010). M. Scott Peck. http://en.wikipedia.org/wiki/M_Scott_Peck.
6. Sheahen, Laura (2005). Interview with M. Scott Peck. *Beliefnet.com*. www.beliefnet.com/faiths/2005
7. Gallagher, Richard F. (2008). A Case of Demonic Possession. *Vox Vocis*. Mar 24. 3,4,10. www.voxvocis.us
8. Sanderson, Alan (1998). Clara-Spirit Releasement Therapy in a Case Featuring Depression and Panic Attacks. *European Journal of Clinical Hypnosis,* 4,4.
9. Wikipedia (2010). James Randi. http://en.wikipedia.org/wiki/Jame_Randi.

10. Stahl, Lesley (2009) Eyewitness: How Accurate is Visual Memory? 60 Minutes. CBS News. July 11.
11. U.S. Department of Justice (1999). *Eyewitness Evidence: A Guide for Law Enforcement Research Report.* October 1999.
12. McBroom, Patricia (1996). A Belief in Protective Illusions Is Good for Children, According to Berkeley Psychologist. *News Release,* 12/16/96.
13. Potok, Mark (2010). Rage on the Right: The Year in Hate and Extremism. *Intelligence Report.* Southern Poverty Law Center, Spring 2010. 137-41.
14. McGuire, Michael, and L. Tiger (2010). Brain Science, God Science: Why Religion Endures. *Skeptical Inquirer* 34-3 May/ June. 35-38
15. Hamer, Dean (2004). *The God Gene: How Faith Is Hardwired into Our Genes.* New York: Anchor Books.
16. Pinker, Steven (1997). *How the Mind Works.* New York: W.W. Norton & Co.
17. Hood, Bruce M. (2009). *Supersense: Why We Believe in the Unbelievable.* New York: Harper Collins.
18. Pandian, Jacob (2001). The Dangerous Quest for Cooperation between Science and Religion. *Skeptical Inquirer* 25-5:28.
19. Campbell, Joseph (1988). *The Power of Myth. A Conversation between Bill Moyers and Joseph Campbell in 1985 and 1986.* Betty Sue Flowers, ed., New York: Doubleday.
20. Taylor, J. Bolte (2008). *My Stroke of Insight: A Brain Scientist's Personal Journey.* New York: Viking Books.
21. Chopra, Deepak (1994). *Journey into Healing: Awakening the Wisdom Within You.* New York: Harmony Book.

REFERENCES

CHAPTER VIII

1. Wikipedia (2010) Loggerhead Sea Turtle. www. wikipedia.org/wiki/Loggerhead_sea_turtle
2. Monarch Butterfly Site: The King of Butterflies— the Monarch Butterfly. www.monarch-butterfly. com.
3. Monarch Butterfly Migration and Overwintering. 02-Feb-2010 http://www.fs.fed.us/monarchbut-terfly/migration/index.shtml.
4. Isaacson, Rupert (2009). *The Horse Boy: A Father's Quest to Heal His Son*. New York: Little Brown & Co.
5. *Diagnostic Criteria from DSM-IV* (2005). Autistic Disorder. Washington, D.C.: The American Psychiatric Association. 57
6. Des Roches Rosa, Shannon (2010). The Horse Boy's Kristin Neff on Autism and Self Compassion. *Moms & Family* (BlogHer Original Post). www.blogher. com/kristin-neff-selfcompassion-autism-parenting-and-horse-boy.
7. Goodall, Jane (1990). *Through a Window: My Thirty Years with the Chimpanzees of Gombe*. Boston: Houghton Mifflin Co.
8. Gibbons, Ann (2010). Chimpanzees Kill for Land. *Science* Now, June 21. http://news.sciencemag. org/sciencenow/2010/06/chimpanzees-kill-for-land.html.etoc.

9. New Perspectives on the West. Sitting Bull, Tatanka-Iotanka (1831-1890). The West Film Project and WETA (2001). PBS Hawaii.

10. Laframboise, Sandra (2008). Dream Catchers. Dancing to Eagle Spirit Society. www.dancing-toeaglespiritsociety.org.

11. Joiner, Thomas (2005). *Why People Die by Suicide*. Cambridge, Mass: Harvard University Press.

12. Kagan, Herman (2006). *The Psychological Immune System: A New Look at Protection and Survival.* Bloomington, Ind.: AuthorHouse.

13. Campbell, Joseph (1988). *The Power of Myth. A Conversation between Bill Moyers and Joseph Campbell in 1985 and 1986.* Betty Sue Flowers, ed. New York: Doubleday.

14. Wikipedia (2010) Metal of Honor. 1. http:// en.wikipedia.org/wiki/Metal_of_Honor.

15. Associated Press (2007). Raymond Murphy Obituary. Medal of Honor Citation, April 10, 2007. www.mishalov.com/murphy-obit.html

16. Wikipedia (2010) List of Military Decorations. http://en.wikipedia.org/wiki/list_of_ military_decorations.

17. Gonalo Arijon (2010). Stranded: The Andes Plane Crash Survivors. Independent Lens. PBS Film. www.pbs.org/independentlens/stranded/film.html.

18. Wikipedia (2010) Wrestling. http://en.wikipedia. org/wiki/wrestling.

19. Wikipedia (2010) Boxing. http://en.wikipedia. org/wiki/boxing.

20. Bentley, Amy (1994). Police Laud Man as 'Hero', Samaritan: Driver Intervened to Stop Woman From Stabbing Her Ex-Boyfriend. *Ventura County Star Free Press*, September 22.

21. Associated Press (1994). The Most Famous Truce in History, Christmas 1914. *Ventura County Star Free Press*, December 12.
22. Wikipedia (2011) Horus. http://en.wikipedia.org/wiki/Horus.
23. Age Mythology Stories (2010). The War between the Titans and the Olympians. April 13. http://agemythologystories. blogspot.com/2010/04/war-between-Titans-and-Olympians.html.
24. Zimbardo, Philip (1992). *Psychology and Life* (Thirteenth Edition). New York: Harper Collins 575.
25. Ibid 600.

www.ingramcontent.com/pod-product-compliance
Lightning Source LLC
Chambersburg PA
CBHW030446290526
45786CB00001B/465